RICHARD BONG

ALSO BY DON KEITH

Chuck Yeager

Torpedo Run

Only the Brave

Arabian Storm

Cuban Deep

Fast Attack

Hunter Killer

The Indestructible Man

Dream On

Dial Dancing

Dangerous Grounds

The Ship That Wouldn't Die

The Amateur Radio Dictionary

Get on the Air . . . Now!

Mattie C.'s Boy

The Spin

Firing Point

Riding the Shortwaves

Undersea Warrior

On the Road to Kingdom Come

We Be Big

War Beneath the Waves

The Ice Diaries

Final Patrol

The Bear

In the Course of Duty

Gallant Lady

Final Bearing

The Forever Season

RICHARD BONG

America's #1 Ace Fighter Pilot of
World War II

DON KEITH

CALIBER

DUTTON CALIBER

an imprint of Penguin Random House LLC
penguinrandomhouse.com

Copyright © 2023 by Don Keith
Penguin Random House supports copyright. Copyright fuels creativity,
encourages diverse voices, promotes free speech, and creates a vibrant culture.
Thank you for buying an authorized edition of this book and for complying with
copyright laws by not reproducing, scanning, or distributing any part of it in
any form without permission. You are supporting writers and allowing
Penguin Random House to continue to publish books for every reader.

DUTTON CALIBER and the D colophon are registered trademarks of
Penguin Random House LLC.

All photos from Army Air Forces/US Air Force archives.

LIBRARY OF CONGRESS CATALOGING-IN-PUBLICATION DATA
has been applied for.

ISBN 9780593187296 (trade paperback)
ISBN 9780593187302 (ebook)

Printed in the United States of America

1st Printing

★ CONTENTS ★

Prologue   xi

One   President Coolidge's Mail Plane   1

Two   "Pinky" and the "Atalanta"   11

Three   Dusty Runways   22

Four   The Tenor in the "Vultee Vibrator"   32

Five   Dirty Laundry   41

Six   Biding Time   51

Seven   Ace of Aces   59

Eight   First Two   70

Nine   "The Swede" Starts to Work   84

Ten   Three Kills in Two Days   94

Eleven   The Competition Heats Up   105

Twelve   Rewarding the Wingman   114

Thirteen   Ten and Eleven   123

Fourteen   Strafing a Croc   130

Fifteen   Foxed at 10,000 Feet   135

Sixteen   Hunting Season   149

Seventeen   Marge   163

Eighteen   "The Flying Circus"   172

Nineteen   Coke and Bedsheets   183

Twenty   "I Had to Shoot Them Down"   190

CONTENTS

Twenty-One   Credit Where Credit Is Due   202

Twenty-Two   PR, Proposal, and a Promise Kept   209

Twenty-Three   The Sharpshooting Instructor   216

Twenty-Four   Happy Skepticism   224

Twenty-Five   The Society of the Bravest of the Brave   231

Twenty-Six   "He Can Be of Great Value to Us Here"   247

Twenty-Seven   "Quite an Airplane"   257

Epilogue   264

★

People driving along Interstate 94 between Milwaukee and Chicago are often amused and intrigued by a big maroon-and-white sign near exit 340. "Bong Recreation Area," it reads. If the motorists decide to tap up Google on their phones, they learn this spot is not really the next innovation in recreational-marijuana use. No, it is an actual state park, named not for a glass smoking pipe but to honor a Wisconsin-born hero of that long-ago conflict World War II.

Most don't bother to dig that deeply. They prefer their initial perception. The state highway department has to replace the sign often because people keep stealing it. And T-shirts sporting a picture of it are strong sellers on the Internet.

That's because most people associate the name with a marijuana pipe, not a man who did what he did more than three quarters of a century ago. Except for World War II or military aviation buffs, few today are even aware of who Richard Ira Bong was or what he did on our behalf.

But they should know. And here is why.

★

PROLOGUE

To be prepared for war is one of the most effective means of preserving peace.
—George Washington

The recording artist Edwin Starr once asked in the lyrics of a hit song, "War, what is it good for?" Then, in answering his own question, he sang, "Absolutely nothing!"

That may not be quite true. Out of war come at least two things besides the obvious death, destruction, and misery.

First, by necessity, there is technological advancement, even if it is usually accomplished in order to kill people and blow things up more effectively than the enemy can.

And second, war gives us unexpected heroes. Men and women who have no idea of what they can do until they are faced with the ultimate challenge.

It is undeniable that war requires and produces technological innovation. As the threat of armed conflict looms, navies, air forces, and armies evaluate and ramp up. Then, once bullets fly, they adapt and modify, based on experience. Those who hesitate or are unable to innovate typically lose. Historian and writer Adrian R. Lewis says, "Without war men would not traverse oceans in hours, travel in space, or microwave popcorn."

The Lockheed P-38 "Lightning" aircraft is a fine case in point. In 1937, with Adolf Hitler remilitarizing Germany despite the terms of the treaty that ended World War I, and with the Empire of Japan boldly and brutally invading China and the Southwest Pacific, the US Army Air Corps made a fateful decision that would eventually play a part in the outcome of the war most believed would never involve the United States. They decided to create a fighter airplane that would be better able to respond to hostilities with either nation. And they would do so despite the strong determination by most—from their commander in chief, President Franklin Roosevelt, on down the chain of command—to never again enter a war that did not directly threaten the borders of the United States.

Air Corps Proposal X-608 was released in February of 1937, only three months after Japan and Germany signed a mutual-defense treaty and five months before Japan invaded China in full force. The detailed document described not only a warplane that did not yet exist but one many experts and engineers felt could not be built. It would defy many of the basic limitations of physical science. It would need to fly at high altitudes and at lightning speeds—better than 360 miles per hour in level flight—and do so while retaining considerable midair maneuverability. It would also have to be capable of climbing to 20,000 feet in less than six minutes after takeoff. This new airplane would necessarily have to carry at least a half ton of armament and ammunition. That would be about twice the load of any other US fighter aircraft that then existed.

The men who concocted those challenging specs had to resort to a bit of chicanery in the wording of their document to accommodate that last specification. By strict Air Corps standards, no fighter or "pursuit aircraft" could carry more than 500 pounds of armor and ordnance. So the desired warbird would be termed in the proposal as an "interceptor," which had no such restrictions, instead of a "fighter."

Forward thinkers in the Air Corps wanted a one-man-crew fighter plane that could escort bombers at high altitude, that had the range to make long runs over vast stretches of water (such as might be required in the Pacific), and yet that would be flexible and fast enough to competitively dogfight with the best of the fighters already being flown by the German Luftwaffe and the Imperial Japanese Navy Air Service.

By most estimates, Proposal X-608 contained the most challenging aircraft design requirements ever submitted. Some of the usual manufacturers simply shook their heads and refrained from making a bid.

The best minds at Lockheed Aircraft in Burbank, California, accepted the challenge. Engineers there quickly realized it would take an aircraft with two engines to accomplish what the Army was looking for. The result was a Frankenstein of an airplane. It would have three main bodies, including twin fuselages to accommodate the two liquid-cooled Allison engines—that specific cooling system was another requirement in the proposal—as well as to support between them the odd-looking tail assembly. Between the two booms, they would hang a shorter central nacelle. That would be where the pilot rode. The plane's guns would also be placed in the nose of that section, in the middle of the aircraft. This eliminated needing to time the firing of the weapons through the propellers and having to consider the angles of deflection and convergence of the ordnance when weapons were mounted farther apart, on the wings of the aircraft.

Range—how far the airplane could fly, do its job, and return to base—remained a prime consideration. The P-38 had an internal fuel capacity of 410 gallons, which amounted to about 450 miles of flight distance. Later, two leakproof, self-sealing, ejectable fuel tanks, each one hung beneath a wing, allowed it to carry additional gas. That extended the range to 2,600 miles. The pilots, though, would need the ability to drop those tanks with a quick-release mechanism when sparring with enemy fighters. With their weight gone, they would be able to do the dives, turns, and climbs necessary to be nimble in a dogfight.

As with other machines developed before and early in the conflict, the P-38 would undergo continued modifications throughout World War II, but that initial challenging proposal resulted in a warplane that appeared to specifically meet the needs of the Allies in Europe. That meant Lockheed had customers from the get-go, even if the US should never become entangled over there. But it also assured an especially effective warplane, as it turned out, in the Pacific Theater of Operations when Japan, with Pearl Harbor, dragged America into the fray.

Colonel Ben Kelsey, a P-38 test pilot, may have best described the warbird's legacy: "[She] would fly like hell, fight like a wasp upstairs, and land like a butterfly."

Never mind that many still thought it to be a funny-looking

bird. The Japanese called the Lightning "one pilot, two airplanes." The Germans were even more descriptive, nicknaming the P-38 "the forked-tail devil."

War necessarily develops something else besides new technology and hardware, though. It creates heroes. Seemingly average men and women who find themselves in challenging or terrible situations amid battle but then do remarkably brave things. So often, those individuals would never have had the chance to become future heroes had they not been presented with the opportunity to demonstrate it. That is often a product of happenstance.

That was the case with a young farm boy from northern Wisconsin named Richard Ira Bong. As chance would have it, he graduated high school and came of age at precisely the time his nation would need him. And he would do what he did in an innovative new airplane, the P-38 Lightning, as if he had been born to pilot one.

Even then, Bong might well have chosen another way to serve his country, had it not been for coincidence. That came when President Calvin Coolidge chose a spot in Superior, Wisconsin, as a summer office and retreat. Any time Coolidge was there, enjoying the cool weather and great fishing, the president's mail was delivered to him each day by an Army airplane. Otherwise, aircraft rarely sullied those rural skies. Eight-year-old Dick Bong looked up from his farm chores to see the Army mail plane flying low over the family's pastures. That sight soon had the boy dreaming of becoming a pilot.

There was one more fortuitous aspect that assured Bong

would become one of those heroes that battle best identifies and confirms. He turned out to be remarkably adept at flying fighter aircraft. Later, one of Bong's instructors at Luke Field near Phoenix, Arizona, pointed out the unassuming young man to a fellow instructor.

"He told me that kid was the finest natural pilot he ever met," the second officer, future US senator and presidential candidate Barry Goldwater, later recalled.

As happened with so many others, wartime allowed Dick Bong to find, hone, and effectively employ his specific skills to help shorten and win the conflict. He would ultimately become his country's top fighter pilot of World War II, its ace of aces, with forty confirmed enemy "kills," and likely just as many more that were not officially verified or that were deliberately gifted by Bong to other pilots. And he would accrue that remarkable score in an aircraft that might not have ever been developed and flown without the very specific needs of a brutal war.

That, of course, is one more thing warfare sometimes creates. A serendipitous matchup of warrior and weapon that gives one side or the other an edge that turns a battle and ultimately wins the war.

In this case, it was a marriage that might never have happened if those Lockheed engineers had not accepted the challenge of building and flying that forked-tail devil to meet the demanding requirements of the Army Air Corps.

Or if that Wisconsin farm boy had not looked up from his chores and watched in awe as President Coolidge's mail plane noisily buzzed past in the deep blue summer skies overhead.

RICHARD BONG

CHAPTER ONE

PRESIDENT COOLIDGE'S MAIL PLANE

In 1896, when Gust Bong decided to move his family from the tiny town of Islingby, Sweden, all the way across the Atlantic Ocean to America, he did what so many other immigrants had done. He left behind his wife and four children—two boys and two girls—with family and friends. For two more years, they would remain in their home in the little Swedish farming village about a hundred miles northwest of Stockholm. But that was only so Gust could find the perfect place for them to settle in their new country. Only then did he send word for them to come join him. And, as it also was with so many immigrants, that "perfect place" would turn out to be much like the one they were leaving behind.

Poplar, Wisconsin, was a farming village with a population of fewer than four hundred souls. It was located about twenty miles down Highway 2 from the bigger towns of Superior, Wisconsin, and Duluth, Minnesota, and only about ten miles from the deep, frigid waters of Lake Superior. Islingby had been close by the Baltic Sea. Also as was the case back home, the earth in their new home was black and fertile, thanks to rich soil dragged south from the Canadian prairies by glaciers during the Ice Age. Gust Bong told his wife and children that he could likely poke an ax handle in the Wisconsin dirt and it would sprout leaves in the warmth of spring.

The people who populated their new environs would be familiar to his family, too. Blond or redheaded, rugged farm folk, almost all Lutheran, and most of them migrants as well from Northern Europe in general and Scandinavia in particular. They were accustomed to the brutal cold and deep snows, and by nature, they rarely complained about them. They worked hard in season to coax crops from the dirt and raise livestock, to keep the cows milked, to log the nearby forests when the snow allowed for the use of sleds, and to take for sustenance the area's plentiful wild game.

Gust Bong's oldest boy, Carl, had just turned seven when the family crossed the ocean and joined their patriarch in Poplar. That was in 1898. And the boy immediately went to work on the farm, as was expected.

After the ferocious winters took their toll on the area roadways, citizens willingly pitched in to make them passable again. For no pay, of course. By the time Carl was in his late teens, that became one of his duties, too. He was well on his way to becoming an old Swedish bachelor—in his early twenties—when he was working one day on Highway 2, the main east–west route across northern Wisconsin. He had stopped to lean on his shovel for a brief rest, but also to watch an attractive girl walking past, as she often did on her way home from school. Dora Bryce was the daughter of another area farmer. Carl eventually got up the nerve to ask if he could walk her home, then later if she would go out on a date with him.

It was the start of a long courtship—she was of Scottish-British heritage, not Scandinavian, and nine years younger than he—but the romance blossomed. The two finally scheduled a wedding in the spring of 1917.

Then, as happened with so many others, a distant war abruptly hijacked their plans. The Great War—later renamed World War I—broke out in Europe. Carl Bong joined the US Army. He was sent to France to serve in the Army Corps of Engineers. The wedding was necessarily postponed until he could win the war and get back home. Nuptials finally took place in July of 1919 in Duluth, and the couple settled in on the Bong farm in Poplar, ready to start their own family.

As was also typical of the place and time, it did not take them long. The first of Carl and Dora's nine children was born on September 24, 1920. It was a boy. They named him Richard Ira Bong. By the time he could walk, he began doing chores, as was expected of him. He also accompanied his father as he hunted and fished, not so much for sport but to put food on the family table. When he turned twelve, Richard got the first gun of his own, a .22 rifle, as a birthday gift. He was soon putting it to good use, supplying venison and other meat. His dad and grandfather had taught him how to shoot and he was good at it, an exceptional marksman, though he did not relish having to climb out of bed hours before sunrise and trudge through snow to be able to shoot at something.

Meanwhile, something else had caught young Richard's interest. To be more accurate, this new curiosity grabbed him and refused to let him go.

When he was about seven and working one day in a field on the farm, he was startled by the approach of a strange sound. It was a motor of some kind. The noise seemed to be coming from the sky, just over the horizon. It was an airplane, a relatively rare sight out there. The boy had seen planes before but certainly not so low and so directly overhead. It was almost as if he could reach up and touch the noisy bird. And he could plainly see the face of the man who piloted the machine as it passed over. That lone, slow, low-flying aircraft coming and going would become a twice-daily attraction for the next month or so, usually about the same time each day. And it completely kidnapped the boy's imagination.

It was, in fact, a US Army plane, and it was delivering mail to, of all people, the president of the United States. Calvin Coolidge, a New Englander, had decided to vacation that year at a private resort on the Brule River at Cedar Island, southeast of Poplar. That allowed him to escape the stifling heat, humidity, and political roiling of Washington, DC, while taking advantage of the area's hunting and speckled trout fishing. The president chose Superior Central High School as his summer White House office. Daily, for most of a month, an Army plane brought the chief executive's mail to the relatively remote outpost. In doing so, it would fly low, directly above the Bong family farm. The pilot had no way of knowing how much he would inspire seven-year-old Dick Bong to become a flier himself.

Not just to be an airplane pilot. He would be a fighter pilot, as Dick informed his best friend, Roger Robinson.

4

The boy worked his way through the relatively small number of books and the well-used encyclopedia at his elementary school library. He read all he could find about airplanes, pilots, and the first serious air-to-air combat that had most recently taken place in the Great War. His dad had told him about Eddie Rickenbacker, the top Allied fighter ace in the war, how "Fast Eddie" had shot down twenty-six enemy aircraft and received the Medal of Honor for his exceptional bravery.

Also, in hushed tones, Carl spun tales of the "Red Baron," the legendary German fighter pilot Manfred von Richthofen, the ace of aces, who had claimed an astonishing eighty victims with his biplane.

Dick's curiosity about aviation was already at a peak when he delved deeper into something that had happened the previous year. In May of 1927, Charles Lindbergh, another former airmail pilot, made his historic solo flight across the Atlantic. The massive media coverage of that signal event ignited interest in aviation among millions of young men and women around the world. That eventually included a fair-haired farm boy in far northern Wisconsin.

As part of this newfound fascination with airplanes, Dick Bong became an avid model builder. When he was not at church, in school, or on the family farm performing his many chores, he spent hours in the bedroom he shared with his brothers, putting together nonflying balsa-wood model airplanes. To get to their beds, his two younger brothers, Carl Jr. and Jim, had to push aside planes that hung by strings from the ceiling while the glue was setting up.

His friend Roger joined Dick in the model building, but

Roger preferred putting together scale replicas of bombers. Dick was far more interested in the few fighter models that were available by mail order. He longed for one of the bigger models— ones that featured an actual gasoline engine that turned the propeller and made it possible to remotely fly the airplane at the end of a length of unspooled wire. There were tantalizing ads for such craft in the pulp magazines and comic books of the time, but they were priced a bit beyond the limits of the Bong family budget.

They were hardly poor, even when the Great Depression set in with a vengeance. In addition to the farm, which did quite well and kept the family fed, Carl Bong had started a road construction and repair business and landed several county contracts. Even so, frugality was a hallmark of the Scandinavians.

Despite his fixation on model airplanes and with his eyes always on the skies, hoping to catch a glimpse of a plane, Dick was a good student and very active in school and church. Though small in stature, he was a fine athlete. In addition, he played clarinet in the high school band, sang in the Lutheran church choir, and joined the 4-H Club. Later on, he did date occasionally, and with his pleasant disposition and easy smile, he was very popular with his classmates. He picked up the nickname "Pinky" because of his pale complexion, but he did not mind it. It was just another sign his classmates liked him. Still, he preferred spending his limited spare time in his room, either reading about airplanes or building scale models of them.

When he began driving, he proved to be adept at mechanical work, too, helping keep the family car running. He did have an unfortunate tendency to push the car or truck faster than his parents preferred. About the only reprimands given to the otherwise well-behaved teenager came after Carl or Dora received reports of his overly aggressive driving.

Poplar High School did not offer a twelfth grade, so for his senior year, Dick had to go all the way up to Superior to earn his high school diploma. Superior Central High School proved to be something of a culture shock. The place had more than four hundred students in the twelfth grade alone, about as many people as the entire population of Poplar. Even so, Dick excelled, becoming something of a big fish in an even bigger pond. He played basketball, baseball, and hockey, continued with the clarinet, and graduated fourteenth in his class academically in the spring of 1938.

Now that high school was over, Bong had decisions to make. Most young men of the time, whether they finished high school or not, simply continued to work on their parents' acreage until they found a mate, married, started a family, and either bought their own plot of land or eventually inherited all or a portion of their home farm. Either way, once a farmer, always a farmer. New grad Dick Bong had higher aspirations.

He determined early in his senior year of high school that, unlike most other males growing up in that area and time, he would go on to college. He chose nearby Superior State Teachers College—now the University of Wisconsin–Superior—a school that had previously trained mostly females for certification as schoolteachers. Fortunately for Dick Bong, they had recently begun to expand their offerings to include a broad-based general education program. That would allow Dick to go to college while continuing to help with the farmwork and his dad's construction business.

There was one driving factor in Bong's decision to attend college. That came from his burning desire to become a military fighter pilot, a goal that had not waned one iota over the years. If anything, it was even stronger by the time he completed high school. And that was even though he still had been no closer physically to an actual full-sized airplane than the one that had flown over the farm with President Coolidge's mail.

In 1938, only officers could be selected for pilot training for the US Army Air Corps. No enlisted men. And no one could become an Army officer without at least two years of postsecondary academic credit. Now Superior State could provide Bong just what he needed—two years of college—so he entered the school's general education program with no intent to earn a degree. He only wanted to accumulate the credits he needed to try to become a flight officer in the Army.

In another example of good timing, the school soon added the perfect program for a would-be pilot. When the US Congress passed the Civil Aeronautics Act of 1938, it authorized, among other things, the establishment of a pilot-training program that could be adopted by colleges across the nation. While ostensibly intended to help create civilian pilots for the rapidly growing aeronautical industry, the program would also prepare a ready pool of fliers for the military should there be a war again. Most knew that if that happened, airplanes would now play a key role.

Under the Civil Aeronautics Act, the government would pay

for a college student to take seventy-two hours of ground school training and thirty-five to fifty hours of flight instruction. Superior State was one of the first schools to offer the program and Dick Bong was one of the first to sign up for it.

At the time, he may or may not have been aware of the ominous rumblings around the planet, thunderclaps that foretold the all-encompassing storm that would soon rage across the globe. Or that this coming maelstrom would make fighter pilots a particularly valuable commodity.

Though he never lacked confidence, there was no way for Dick to even know if he had what it took to become a combat pilot. Or if he could learn to fly a plane. All he knew was that he wanted to try. He could drive cars fast. He understood how machines worked and how airplanes could fly. He had glued together plenty of scale models of fighter planes. That gave him some concept of how they did what they did. But there was no way he could have known if he had the skills needed to buzz wildly about the sky, all alone in the cockpit of a warplane, dodging enemy aviators who were firing live ammunition at him. All while trying to stay in the air and draw a steady bead on that darting, zooming, and determinedly deadly adversary.

But he was certain about one thing. This was what he wanted to do.

Bong was likely not aware either that forward thinkers in the American military were preparing for war, even if most of the government—and many prominent individuals, including one of the boy's heroes, Charles Lindbergh—had vowed there would be no participation by the United States in any conflict between nations on the other side of the world. But others felt it prudent to prepare, just in case. Part of that preparation was designing and testing weaponry to fight the kind of war the military was anticipating.

Submarines. Tanks. Ships. Beach landing craft. Airplanes. Each more sophisticated and technologically advanced—and deadly—than anything that had preceded it.

Even the current president, Franklin D. Roosevelt, who had remained staunchly isolationist as Europe once again went to war and the Japanese expanded their empire in the Pacific, went before Congress on May 16, 1940, requesting they create funding to build fifty thousand warplanes. Just in case.

Equally important, those who had chosen to prepare for another global conflagration were also developing curricula and designating training facilities for the men (and some few women) who would be called upon to test, maintain, helm, drive, fight, and fly that specialized machinery.

It would soon prove fortuitous for his nation that "Pinky" Bong was hell-bent on becoming a fighter pilot instead of a bean, alfalfa, and cattle farmer. That there was a program to prepare kids from Middle America for warbird cockpits. That the US Army Air Corps had already developed specs and would soon test-fly the P-38 Lightning.

And that the plane would be the perfect fighter aircraft for the young dreamer's unique—but still unrecognized—talents.

CHAPTER TWO

"PINKY" AND THE "ATALANTA"

Two months after Richard Bong graduated from Superior Central High School, Lockheed Aircraft began construction of the P-38 "interceptor" combat aircraft. The company had landed the contract to build the plane for the US Army Air Corps with their response to the rather demanding Proposal X-608. By the time World War II ended, more than 10,000 various versions of the birds had been built and put into service.

To maintain secrecy, Lockheed did initial construction on the plane at a remote assembly plant in Southern California they had dubbed the "Skunk Works." The first completed version of the aircraft, designated as XP-38 ("X" for "experimental"), was flown by test pilot Ben Kelsey, one of the original authors of the Proposal X-608 proposal document. That occurred on January 27, 1939. That was just as Dick Bong was beginning his second semester in college while still working full-time on the farm and with his dad's road construction company. The test flights of the unusual-looking aircraft were so impressive that Kelsey proposed a rather radical way to demonstrate its practical capabilities as well as to show how successfully Lockheed had met the specified needs of the Army Air Corps.

Range and speed would be two of the primary attributes of the P-38. What better way to demonstrate them than to make a cross-country trip from Los Angeles to Wright Field in Dayton, Ohio—especially since Lockheed and the Air Corps had already planned to move this, their only working copy of the plane, to Wright Field for further observations at the Army's aircraft test facility there?

The commander of the US Army Air Corps at the time, General Henry "Hap" Arnold, was enthusiastic about the plan. However, he suggested they take it one spectacular step further. Why not go coast-to-coast, all the way to New York City, to show what the Lightning could do? And in the process, break the existing speed record for a flight from one coast to the other.

That became the plan.

On February 11, 1939, one month before Adolf Hitler's German forces invaded and claimed the part of Czechoslovakia they had not already "annexed," Kelsey climbed into the XP-38 aircraft bearing serial number one in California and set out for New York. He was so confident that he could beat the existing cross-continent record that he took it relatively easy, especially while landing for two fuel stops along the way. The second stop was at Wright Field, where General Arnold was among those waiting to greet Kelsey. Arnold urged the pilot to "not spare the horses," to go top speed on to his destination at Mitchel Field in

Hempstead, New York. Kelsey obliged, reaching a speed of 420 miles per hour for much of the final leg of his journey.

The previous record had been set in January 1937 by business tycoon and movie mogul Howard Hughes, piloting an H-1 Racer designed and built by his company, Hughes Aircraft. The plane was designed to do little else than go fast. It took him seven hours and twenty-eight minutes flying nonstop from Burbank, California, to Newark, New Jersey. By the time Kelsey left Ohio, he was on track to beat that record by almost an hour.

However, when the XP-38 neared the airport on western Long Island, the controller in the tower at Mitchel Field, unaware of the significance of the approaching aircraft or that a record was at stake, put Kelsey into a holding pattern behind unusually heavy air traffic in the area. As Kelsey circled, awaiting permission to land, he realized something was wrong. It was later determined that ice had formed in the plane's carburetor, cutting off the flow of fuel. The XP-38 had not yet been tested at such slow speeds and in frigid wintry air. The pilot had to crash-land short of the field, destroying in the process the only '38 in existence at the time. Fortunately, Kelsey was able to walk away from the wreckage.

Still, most authorities honored Kelsey's flight duration—seven hours and one minute, not counting time on the ground for refueling—as a new record, one that would stand for six years. And the Army Air Corps was impressed enough with the plane's performance that they promptly placed an order for thirteen of them.

Those next models to be built would have quite a few differences from the experimental version that crashed at Hempstead.

The major one was that the rotation of the propeller blades was reversed, resulting in the aircraft being remarkably stable in flight. That would make the P-38 a good platform not only for shooting at enemy planes but also for photoreconnaissance work.

A more troubling issue was a tendency for the pilot to lose control of the plane during high-altitude dives as it approached a speed of Mach 0.68. The tail would begin to flutter violently, and the nose pointed downward no matter how hard the pilot pulled back on the stick. After several pilots bailed out under such conditions, others learned to ride out the stall until they were in less thin air and able to employ elevator trim to help regain control. The problem still existed, even as Lockheed rushed to deliver to the Army the next order of sixty-five P-38s in September 1941. They also had to fill an even bigger requisition from the British and French, who were already at war with Germany. Those air forces were desperate for any weapon to counter Hitler and his Luftwaffe.

However, the loss-of-control issue with the airplane understandably gave it something of a bad reputation, even if it was otherwise a significant weapon. The British ultimately canceled much of its original order for the P-38s when one of their Royal Air Force test pilots flew one in California and experienced first-hand the high-altitude stall. Fortunately for Lockheed, that was about the time of Pearl Harbor, and they found a suddenly very motivated buyer in the US Army Air Forces. (The US Army Air Corps officially became the US Army Air Forces on June 20, 1941, as part of a major reorganization of the Army. It would then become its own service branch, the United States Air Force, in September 1947.)

Despite the problems, the P-38 in its various modified forms would eventually serve its users well, including when the US was dragged into the war on December 7, 1941. Pilots learned how to work through the high-speed-stall issue even as other quirks of the plane were observed and corrected. That, of course, was to be expected. It was the case with most technology required by the war effort, from tanks to submarines to carriers to airplanes. Once the equipment was in the field and employed against the enemy, problems or needs were discovered and noted. Updates and fixes were common and constant.

The next-worse issue with the P-38 resulted from the modification to the propeller rotation direction. Generally, having two engines was a big advantage, especially while operating the plane in the Pacific Theater, where mission distances were greatest. The loss of an engine was not necessarily fatal if a second working one was already running and available. The Lightning flew relatively well on one engine.

Not so, however, if the failure occurred on takeoff. Should that happen in most other aircraft, pilots had always been trained to go to full throttle on the remaining motor to try to maintain airspeed and thus be able to climb away from the unforgiving ground. But with the P-38, such a maneuver could cause the plane to yaw violently in the direction of the dead engine. When that happened, and with the airplane still close to the ground on takeoff, it flipped over onto its side or top and crashed, often with fatal results, since the pilot had no opportunity to bail out.

Until much later in the war, the answer to this problem became more of a training point than a design flaw to be corrected.

Should a Lightning's engine fail on takeoff, pilots could avoid a crash by simply reducing power on the working one. Then they could achieve level flight and climb higher above the ground. Though counterintuitive, the maneuver worked.

Another issue—and one that limited the plane's use in Europe—was the lack of cockpit heating and cooling. At higher altitudes, the pilots faced debilitating cold in an already frigid climate. In the Pacific, the cockpits were fine at altitude but very hot when flying low. But that was more a matter of pilot comfort than something that limited the aircraft's usefulness in that part of the world.

There would be other key modifications during the war based on experience and, sometimes, failure. A big addition was the introduction of auxiliary drop fuel tanks, which allowed the plane to dramatically increase its operating range, a key advantage in the vast Pacific. Along with the wing and fuselage fuel tanks, these drop tanks were designed to be self-sealing, so taking a bullet in one of them did not necessarily cause it to leak dry or catch fire.

There was one early modification that had no effect on the aircraft's performance but almost certainly helped its eventual image. That change was the plane's name. When the British placed their original order, they nicknamed the bird "Lightning." Lockheed, who often dipped into Greek mythology for product names, had previously settled on "Atalanta." In Greek mythology, she became a huntress after being abandoned by her father and raised in the wild by a she-bear. But Lockheed ceded to the customer's wishes. The P-38 would be the "Lightning" for the rest of its time in use, even if the Royal Air Force never did use the airplane.

The very first P-38s put into service were actually used as photoreconnaissance aircraft by the Royal Australian Air Force, beginning in April of 1942. The British and later the US would also use them for such work in Africa and the Mediterranean region in addition to serving as fighters. The Army later estimated that 90 percent of all aerial reconnaissance film taken during the war in Europe was captured by smooth-flying P-38s.

In May of 1942, two dozen Lightnings went to work in the Aleutian Islands of Alaska, patrolling their 1,200-mile length, typically in terrible weather. On August 9, two P-38s happened upon a pair of Japanese Kawanishi H6K "Mavis" flying boats and promptly shot them down, making them the first Japanese planes destroyed by Lightnings.

Only five days later, a P-38 operating out of Iceland encountered a Focke-Wulf Fw-200 "Condor" over the Atlantic and, along with a pilot in another type of fighter, attacked and shot it down. That was the first Luftwaffe plane taken down by a P-38.

The plane would prove to be best suited for and most valuable in the Pacific. America's top three ace fighter pilots did all their damage in P-38s. Once Lockheed was able to fill the need, and until North American Aviation could produce significant numbers of the equally effective P-51 Mustang single-engine combat aircraft, the Lightning became the Army's primary long-range fighter in use against the Japanese.

As he matriculated at Superior State, Richard Bong would not have known that the ride in which he would one day make history had been proposed, the contract for its creation awarded, and the first models built and tested. Nor could he have known when he initially enrolled in college that the P-38 would soon be constructed in large numbers and a school program introduced that would let him develop the skills required to put that remarkable airplane to use.

The requirements of war would result in both the creation of advanced technology and the discovery and training of those who could take advantage of it.

At its inception, the Civilian Pilot Training Program planned on turning out 11,000 would-be pilots per year and, ironically, was modeled on similar initiatives in Germany and Italy. Participating colleges were required to be located within ten miles of an airport that had a runway at least 1,800 feet long in a flat area no less than 300 feet wide. That airfield had to have landing approaches permitting a 20:1 glide path. Students were required to pass a Civil Aeronautics Administration flight physical. The law creating the program also specified that it be made available to African American students. In 1939, six predominantly Black schools began training pilots. They included Tuskegee Institute in Alabama, where many of the famous Tuskegee Airmen began their careers as military pilots with the CPT Program.

On September 27, 1940, Japan, Germany, and Italy formally signed the Tripartite Pact, creating what would be called the Axis alliance. The treaty declared that an attack on any of the three would be an attack on all of them.

Three days before the formal creation of that ominous relationship, on "Pinky" Bong's twentieth birthday, September 24, 1940, the college sophomore climbed into an airplane and left

Earth behind for the very first time. It was everything he expected it to be. He could not wait to fly again. He had already passed the first major hurdle. By law, only ten students from each ground school class could be selected to advance to flight school. That selection would be based on competitive scores. Bong was among the ten in his group to move on and train to be a pilot by flying a plane and eventually soloing.

The aircraft in which he took that initial flight was nothing at all like the P-38 Lightning. It was a bright yellow Piper Cub, a single-engine craft that could carry a pilot and one passenger. Even with a stiff tailwind, it could barely make 90 miles per hour and typically cruised at about 75 miles per hour. But it did leave the ground and became airborne. It could climb to a maximum operating altitude of about 11,500 feet. Bong kept reminding himself that was more than two miles high!

He also knew that what he had been taught in ground school and what he had learned in that canary yellow airplane would be all he needed to qualify to take the next step. He would not yet have earned a bachelor's degree in college, but he would have the credit hours necessary to enlist in the US Army and enter their pilot-training program. The Civilian Pilot Training Program experience would, he felt, give him a leg up on others with the same idea. He would already be a licensed pilot.

What Bong did not consider was that more than 9,000 men—and some women, since one of the ten students who were selected to advance to CPT Program flight training at each college or university offering the program could be female—had pretty much the same idea that he did. Plus, those who had graduated from schools that did not offer CPT but were otherwise qualified to become military officers and pilots could apply. Admission to the program to become a military flight officer would not be automatic.

But as it happened, both the Army and Navy were welcoming as many would-be pilots as they could sign up. First, they knew there would be a high attrition rate in the program. Pilot training would be rigorous. Many would drop out. Many others would fail. And tragically, more than a few would die in trainer aircraft crashes. Those were the cold, hard facts. The Army would need as many qualified trainees as it could get to meet the needs of a possible war.

There were by then growing indications that the US might enter the conflict after all. On October 16, 1940, military draft registration was ordered to begin in the United States. Again, just in case. Most still felt—or hoped—there would be no United States troop involvement in the war that was already boiling over in Europe and simmering in the Far East.

When the draft began, Dick Bong did his duty and registered, but he was confident he would not be conscripted, even if his country should become embroiled in a war. He intended to beat them to the punch by enlisting once he earned the required academic credits by completing the current semester.

Toward the end of October of 1940, President Franklin Roosevelt, campaigning for reelection, stated flatly that he would not "send any of our boys to war." This even though in the Atlantic, German U-boats were attacking US vessels that were carrying supplies and weapons to Great Britain. On November 5, 1940, President Roosevelt won an unprecedented third term.

On January 23, 1941, aviation pioneer Charles Lindbergh

testified before the US Congress and again made a strong case for avoiding any involvement in the conflicts in Europe or Asia. Instead, he urged, the United States should seek a neutrality pact with Adolf Hitler. Many who once considered him a hero now denounced him as a Nazi sympathizer.

It was also in January of 1941 that Dick Bong's grades from the previous term were posted. Ever the good student, he had no worries. Once he had a transcript verifying that he had successfully earned the required college credit, he went down to the recruitment center and enlisted in the US Army Air Corps Aviation Cadet Program. He passed the physical examination and was accepted for pilot training. However, he would have to continue helping on the farm and, when the spring thaw began, work with the road crew. He would not be required to report for duty until more than four months later, on May 29, in Wausau, Wisconsin. It was only the beginning of a long, frustrating process.

From Wausau, he would be sent west to a place where the terrain and weather were perfect for teaching young men how to fly. But it would be a year before Bong climbed into the cockpit of his first Lockheed P-38 Lightning. And just a short while after when he did something in that airplane that came close to getting him thrown out of the Army Air Forces before he could even engage in his first dogfight.

The stunt enraged his commanding officer mightily. At the same time, Bong's piloting skills in pulling it off so impressed his boss that the young flier quickly became one of his personal favorites for all of World War II.

CHAPTER THREE

DUSTY RUNWAYS

The extensive and intense training US pilots received prior to being dispatched to war zones would give them a considerable advantage over enemy fliers. Early on, though, Axis pilots—and especially those of Hitler's Luftwaffe—were well prepared. By the time the United States entered the war in December 1941, those who flew for the Führer and the Japanese Emperor had far more real-world combat experience than the Americans. The Army Air Forces had practically none except for a few Great War pilots who had flown radically different aircraft to victory two decades earlier. Most of them were too old to go to war again. Even so, the AAF was determined that America would have not only the best warplanes, but also the best-trained crew members to man them. Again, it was General Hap Arnold who spearheaded the effort.

This meant months of intense and specific training for would-be pilots. And that was maddening for such hard chargers as Richard Bong, those who seemed to be natural combat pilots the first time they climbed into a trainer cockpit. Despite that, everyone had to follow the same schedule as their cohorts, including those who might not be blessed with inherent talent.

Resulting frustration often led to high jinks or overly aggressive behavior in the skies. Sometimes it was destructive. Even the otherwise straight-arrow Dick Bong would ultimately participate in the shenanigans.

Once town fathers in California, Arizona, Nevada, and Texas noticed the military was establishing flight training schools in locations offering flat geography and sunny, clear weather, they found new value in undeveloped, dusty, tumbleweed-strewn land. Alert entrepreneurs also saw opportunity in the demand for Army flight schools. In 1939, the Army Air Corps cadet pilot programs had the capacity to turn out only about 750 graduates a year. Those who anticipated another world war knew something had to be done to prepare for a conflict that would require strong airpower. It was likely a good portion of any war would be fought as much in the skies as in the trenches.

One of the businessmen who saw a chance to cash in was John Gilbert "Tex" Rankin, a bigger-than-life aerobatic pilot, barnstormer, crop duster, flight instructor, and air racer who had already set several early flying records. Rankin had pioneered methods of flight training and even flown for Hollywood film productions. He had taught such celebrities as Jimmy Stewart and Errol Flynn how to fly and become licensed pilots. Through his contacts, Rankin learned the Department of Defense was looking to award contracts to qualified bidders to operate schools for an anticipated influx of cadets. With his background, expertise, and notoriety, Rankin readily won a contract and went to work to locate the best spot to conduct such training.

California's San Joaquin Valley offered what Rankin would tout as the best flying conditions weather-wise in the entire United States. Clouds, fog, and rain were a rarity. That meant that students and their instructors could be in the sky practically all day every day. A plot of acreage in what was mostly tabletop-flat farmland eight miles southeast of the town of Tulare also offered the near-perfect location for multiple runways and buildings to house the facility. That included barracks and drill fields where recruits would be taught to march in formation and could do "PT," physical training. There were few trees or other obstructions. The only things that had to be relocated when construction started were rocks, jackrabbits, and scrub brush.

Rankin Aeronautical Academy and Rankin Field hosted its first students in February of 1941, even as the recently enlisted Dick Bong, back in Wisconsin, impatiently awaited his induction into the Air Corps and assignment to cadet school. The school at Tulare was one of what would eventually be sixty-two civilian-owned training facilities. They would provide basic flight training for almost a million and a half military pilots who would one day crew fighters, bombers, and all types of planes used by the Army during World War II. Rankin Aeronautical and Rankin Field at Tulare would do their share, graduating almost 11,000 pilots over the next four and a half years. That number included twelve World War II aces. (A pilot was designated as being an "ace" once he collected five confirmed "kills" of enemy aircraft.)

Flight schools like Rankin's were part of a massive ramp-up in personnel in the Army Air Corps to go along with the sweeping reorganization of the US Army that was completed in June of 1941. In 1939, the number serving in the Army Air Corps had doubled over the previous decade to more than 23,000. But a mere two years later, when the Air Corps became the US Army Air Forces, more than 152,000 people served as part of the new entity. And that number would swell to about a half million during the first six months of World War II.

As he awaited his marching orders, Dick Bong had to know the service branch in which he had enlisted was exploding. And his feet itched to get going. He took advantage of what opportunity there was to climb back into that bright yellow Piper Cub and get some seat time. It only whetted his appetite and fueled his frustration. All the while, he was hearing about the training aircraft the Air Corps was using at all those new flight schools. There were a few mentions in the newspapers of new fighter aircraft in development. Planes he would soon be piloting once he was a flight officer.

Then, finally, the orders came. Though he had tried not to speculate, he assumed he would be assigned to one of the new cadet schools springing up all over the middle part of the country. There were several in Arkansas, Missouri, and Oklahoma, not that far away. There were many more in Florida, Texas, Alabama, and Mississippi. But when his orders arrived, he was told to report to the Army's induction facility in Wausau, Wisconsin, 200 miles downstate, where he would climb onto a southbound train with other enlistees. Southbound because he would ride all the way to Chicago before transferring over to a westbound train headed for a place whose name he was unsure how to pronounce.

Tulare. Tulare, California. In the San Joaquin Valley. A facility called Rankin Field that had only been in business a few months and had recently graduated its first class.

No matter. They had an aviation school there, with runways and trainer airplanes and flight instructors who could teach him what he needed to know to be a combat fighter pilot. Once settled in for the long train ride into the setting sun, Bong decided that he would simply sit back and enjoy the scenery. He wrote his family he intended to make the trip west a grand adventure. At least he was finally off to do precisely what he wanted to do. There was never a doubt in his mind about being successful at it.

Bong was not well traveled. This would be the longest journey so far in his young life. He and his family had taken one camping trip all the way out to Yellowstone National Park. That had occurred between Dick's sophomore and junior years in high school. Summer vacations were difficult for the Bongs. That was usually peak time for tending the crops. Taking a week or two off then was a rare thing. The boy's other longest trips came when he traveled cross-state a couple of times to Milwaukee.

Whether he could pronounce its name or not, Tulare immediately felt familiar to him when he stepped off the train there on June 2, 1941. It was not near any large city. It was farm country. Even if there were no mountains, no deep, cold lakes, or even many trees, it was much like home in other ways. All the dairy farms, rows of crops stretching far into the distance, and acres and acres of hayfields made the transition relatively easy for him.

The weather was certainly different, much drier and warmer

than he was accustomed to. And there was dust everywhere. Still, even before the train stopped, he could smell the rich soil in the fields of lettuce, and the fragrant blooms on the trees in the valley's vast walnut and pistachio orchards. He liked the place immediately, and even more when he looked up to see a formation of Boeing-Stearman PT-13 Kaydet training aircraft passing noisily overhead.

One thing the young trainee was not ready for was the boot camp atmosphere he would experience. He wanted to learn to fly combat aircraft. But he also had to be taught military discipline, marching, and all that went with being an officer in the US Army. That meant reveille before sunrise, physical training on the hot, dusty parade grounds, classroom training to learn military procedure and protocol, then, anytime they were not in an airplane or in class, more marching and exercising in the unrelenting sun. Bong's Scandinavian skin was quickly chapped by the wind and blistered by the sun. His fellow trainees soon revived his nickname of "Pinky."

He was happiest when he was flying. He would spend many hours in his trainer, the PT-13 Kaydet, the aircraft in which thousands of would-be Army and Navy pilots learned basic skills. The PT-13 did not resemble a fighter or bomber, but it had a stick, a propeller, flaps, and wings. All the basics that other aircraft had. Manufactured by Boeing, who had bought the Stearman Aircraft Company shortly before the Kaydet was introduced, the PT-13 was a biplane—two wings up front, one above and one below the fuselage—with two seats, one behind the other, in open cockpits just behind the top wing. The wings were made with wood framing covered with fabric. The fuselage consisted of a welded steel framework, also covered with fabric. Later models were designated as PT-17 and PT-18 but the only significant difference between the three was the type of engine installed in each.

Each engine produced about 200 horsepower, the plane could reach a speed of about 120 miles per hour, and it could operate up to an altitude of approximately 11,000 feet. The Army Air Corps placed the first order for the biplane in 1935. By the time the last one rolled off the assembly line in 1945, more than 10,000 Kaydets had been delivered and tens of thousands of Army and Navy pilot trainees had cut their flying teeth in them. They were seen as remarkably forgiving of rookie mistakes, almost indestructible, and extremely reliable. Many of them were later used as crop dusters and to perform stunts at air shows. Estimates are that as many as a thousand of them are still regularly flying today.

For Dick Bong, except for more wind in the face in the open cockpit, the Stearman was not that much different from the Piper Cub in which he first learned to fly. Within his first few excursions out over the San Joaquin Valley, he was doing aerobatics, loops, and other tricks, sometimes to the horror but sometimes the delight of his ride-along instructors. Regardless of their reactions, each agreed this Wisconsin farm boy could pilot an airplane.

At the same time, Bong became even more convinced he was where he was supposed to be as he steered that biplane through the sparse, wispy clouds above Tulare. He was always disappointed when it came time to set her back down on the dusty runway to give some other trainee a chance to soar.

The other primary training regimen at Rankin Field was not nearly so enjoyable. By the time they finished all the marching and exercising, went to class, had some seat time in a Stearman, gobbled up mess hall chow, and filed into the barracks each evening, it was already time for "Taps." There was nothing else for the exhausted trainees to do but hit the rack and get ready for the early wake-up call. Then they would do it all again.

Leave time was a rarity. Weekends were just days reserved for more training. Even if there was a chance for a night or weekend off, there was no place to go for some fun. Bakersfield and Fresno were the closest cities, and they were an hour or more hitchhike away. There were only a few rough-and-tumble bars down the road in Tulare. Dick had never been much for bars anyway, and he seldom took a drink. Truth was, the local customers in those joints did not necessarily welcome the young Army trainees, either.

There were a couple of other harsh surprises for Bong. Since the Army was feeding and clothing him, and there was little else on which he expected to spend money, he sent home to his mother most of his monthly pay so she could bank it for him. He would use those savings after he was out of the service and ready to settle down back in Wisconsin. Likely on his own farm with a good Lutheran girl for a wife. But then he learned he would be required to take a third of that payday each month and give it to the Army to cover the cost of his room and board.

The other shocker came when he learned just how long the whole flight training process was going to take. First, he would be stationed there at Rankin Field for ten weeks. Ten long weeks of flying, marching, going to class, doing jumping jacks, and, hopefully, flying some more. If he made the grade in Tulare, not only as a pilot but also as a soldier, and if he did not auger his Stearman into a tomato field somewhere and kill himself, he would graduate from primary training and advance to the next phase. That would require another twenty weeks of basic and advanced training. Should he survive that and successfully meet the requirements of his instructors and the Army, he would ultimately be commissioned as a second lieutenant, receive his pilot wings, and then move on to still more flight training, but of a more specialized nature.

Of course, if he did not make it—yet managed not to kill himself in one of those Stearmans—he would not be kicked out of the service and sent home. No, the Army still had dibs on him. He had voluntarily enlisted. Should he wash out at any point during those thirty weeks, he would lose his chance to be an officer. Most likely, he would be sent to the infantry or some other branch of the Army that needed a large number of foot soldiers. There he would be issued a helmet, a rifle, and a combat backpack, earthbound for any war that might break out.

Dick Bong had no intention of washing out. Or of augering in. (One of the first things he learned was that the trainees never used the word "crash." They preferred the term "augering in.") He was confident he would make the grade and then have some say-so in what kind of aircraft he would fly for Uncle Sam. He remained fixated on being a combat fighter pilot as he had since his airplane-model-building days. Oh, if he ended up flying bombers or some other type of airplane, or spent the war taxiing generals about, he would still do his best for his country. He was, however, determined to spend those thirty difficult weeks showing those who mattered that he had been born to be a fighter jockey.

Early in his stint at Rankin Field, he studied the calendar on the wall of his barracks. There was little joy. Thirty weeks was a long time. He had arrived in Tulare on June 2. Even if all went according to plan, it would be January before he earned his commission and pinned on his pilot wings. That long before he could move on to train to become a fighter pilot.

Thirty weeks. More than half a year.

He knew lots could happen between June 1941 and January 1942 to alter the flight path of young Richard Ira Bong.

CHAPTER FOUR

THE TENOR IN THE "VULTEE VIBRATOR"

A ttrition was always something to be accounted for, from the inception of the Civilian Pilot Training Program all the way through the newly established Army pilot schools. Numbers mattered because as many as half of the early classes washed out. Or crashed their Stearmans, ending their training and sometimes their lives.

Despite the hours of PT he had to endure each morning and the seemingly endless time spent each afternoon in ground school in those stifling classrooms, Dick Bong excelled. That was especially true when he was in the air in the front seat of one of those Kaydets, an impressed instructor watching from the seat behind him. Yes, even in this very basic aircraft and while performing the most rudimentary maneuvers, the trainee from Wisconsin obviously possessed skills most others did not.

On June 25, 1941, just over three weeks after he stepped off the train in Tulare, California, Bong successfully completed his initial solo flight in one of the biplanes. That was also five days after the reorganization of the US Army that created the separate Army Air Forces with General Henry "Hap" Arnold in command. And with international tensions coming to a boil, Bong's solo came about a week and a half after the US government ordered frozen all German and Italian assets in American banks. The embassies and consulates of those two countries were closed and their diplomats were kicked out of the United States. It was also three days after Hitler shocked the world by launching Operation Barbarossa, a massive and brutal attack against Russia, despite an existing pact between the nations agreeing not to go to war with each other. And Dick's solo came on the very same day Russian bombers attacked Helsinki in then-German ally Finland, a neighbor of Sweden, the country in which Dick Bong's father, Carl, was born and from which he migrated to the US.

None of this changed Bong's trajectory or attitude. He pressed on, determined to be the best trainee in his class to improve his chances of being selected for fighter training. Once he had soloed, the only difference he noticed in his everyday life was that the newer trainees who were arriving every week by the busload now called him "sir," just as he had so recently done with those who were only a few weeks ahead of him in the rotation. Three weeks in and he was now an old-timer.

He relished the opportunity to fly the Kaydet on his own, zooming low over the asparagus fields and foothills of the Sierra Nevada Mountains and sometimes venturing out to within view of the Pacific—pushing the 500-mile range of the Stearman for the round trip—to get a glimpse of that vast ocean. He wrote home that he was not especially impressed. It mostly reminded him of Lake Superior.

Time did seem to pass more quickly once he soloed. Before he knew it, his ten weeks at Rankin Aeronautical Academy were up. Rumors were that his class would go to one of the several Army Air Forces bases in Texas for the next phase. However, at the last minute, they were redirected about 75 miles south of Tulare to Gardner Army Airfield in Taft, California. Over the previous months, three asphalt runways had been hastily carved from agricultural fields there. The 528th School Squadron had officially been transferred to Taft on June 2, the same day Dick Bong arrived in Tulare. Buildings were put up quickly and construction was declared complete on July 21, about a month after Bong soloed in the Stearman, and less than a week before the United States—along with New Zealand, Australia, and Great Britain—also froze the financial assets of the Empire of Japan in retaliation for its aggression in China, Southeast Asia, and the Southwest Pacific.

At its height, Gardner had its own hospital, a forty-acre sewage plant, nine administration buildings, four mess halls, thirty-seven barracks, officers' quarters, a chapel, and six other auxiliary runways around the area. By the time the base was closed in January 1945, it had offered instruction to more than 3,000 soldiers (mostly mechanics and other aircraft support personnel) and almost 9,000 pilot trainees. Crashes claimed the lives of thirty-seven pilots and instructors over that period of time, but that was one of the best safety records of any of the air bases around the country. Notable graduates from the training program there would include, in addition to Richard Bong, Charles "Chuck" Yeager, who would be an ace in Europe during the war and become the first man to fly a plane faster than the speed of sound, and football star and future TV sportscaster Tom Harmon.

Bong easily passed his sixty-hour flight test in Tulare on August 11 and received orders to report to Gardner nine days later, on August 20. He had written to his family that if he ended up in Texas for the next twenty weeks, he might have time to visit home before he reported to the new base. Now that was not to be. He would necessarily have to be on base at Tulare to climb on the bus with the rest of his class for the move down to Taft. He did spend a few days in Los Angeles with a classmate who hailed from there. That gave him the chance to see some of the tourist attractions as well as to get a more close-up view of the Pacific Ocean. He remained unimpressed.

The scenery around Taft was different in some ways from the San Joaquin Valley. Not from the ground or in the air. There were plenty of crop fields, some right up to the edges of the runways, and considerable dust, but with the addition of acres of oil rigs pumping away. Before he arrived, Bong knew he would be moving up in terms of the trainer aircraft he would be flying. He was excited about that because the two-seat Vultee BT-13 Valiant, with its wings beneath the fuselage and its enclosed cockpit, looked much more like a fighter plane than the Stearman biplane. He also knew it had a far more powerful engine, roughly twice the horsepower of the Stearman. It was faster with a top speed of almost 200 miles per hour. It was also heavier than the primary trainer he had flown for the past ten weeks. He knew much more would be asked of the trainees in this bird, including conducting instrument-guided night landings and having to learn to use its two-way radio to communicate with the ground and other aircraft. And do all that while practicing loops, rolls, and rudimentary midair combat with one another.

He had also heard of the negatives associated with the Vultee. The plane required the pilot to operate landing flaps using a hand crank attached to a cable. Its landing gear was not retractable. The Valiant also had an annoying—and sometimes dangerous—proclivity for shimmying violently when approaching stall speed. For that reason, the BT-13 had long since been nicknamed the "Vultee Vibrator."

Still, it was an airplane and Bong was ready to fly it. The rest of the training regimen at Gardner was not so enjoyable. The physical and military training at Tulare had been conducted by civilian contractors. At Gardner, there were Army drill instructors. Bong was certain their orders were to drive every possible trainee right out of the service, what with all their yelling and constant verbal harassment. Ground school was more challenging, too. Why did a combat pilot need to know so much algebra anyway? He believed strongly that seat time—zooming over the oil fields and nearby Buena Vista Lake while practicing combat maneuvers and emergency procedures—offered more opportunity to learn how to be a wartime pilot. Though often frustrated, he persevered.

Bong made his successful solo flight in the Valiant on September 3. That was the day before an incident in the Atlantic

Ocean brought the United States much closer to entering the war in Europe. It was on September 4 that the destroyer USS *Greer* (DD-145) became the first US warship to be fired upon by German naval forces. A U-boat launched multiple torpedoes at the ship. All missed, but the incident was a major turning point leading up to war. A week later, in one of his "Fireside Chat" radio broadcasts, President Roosevelt announced to America that he had issued a shoot-on-sight order against any German vessel that dared fire on a US ship, military or not.

Bong did have a bit of social life once he got to Taft. At Tulare, he and his fellow trainees enjoyed USO dances. There were more local restaurants, too, with fare they considered superior to what the Army cooks offered at the base mess hall. That was about it. It was simply too far to regularly go to a place more interesting or fun.

On the other hand, Taft was only about a hundred miles from Los Angeles. When Bong and the other pilots got weekend passes, they would pile into whatever cars were available and head for the bright lights. That proximity worked both ways, too. Famous entertainers from LA often came up to Gardner to put on shows for the personnel there. That included Bob Hope and Duke Ellington. Cowboy movie star Joel McCrea donated money to construct a swimming pool on the base and enjoyed driving up from Hollywood to hang out with the pilot trainees. Johnny Weissmuller was there for the pool's dedication and even performed his famous Tarzan yell for the men. Hope, Edgar Bergen, Jack Benny, and Eddie Cantor did live radio broadcasts from the base theater with the audience mostly made up of pilot trainees.

Bong also joined classmates to form a vocal quartet. He sang the tenor parts. And according to reports, he sang them very well. The group traveled around the area putting on performances as a way of thanking the locals for their hospitality. They even made several appearances on radio stations in the region.

While Bong demonstrated exceptional flying ability, he did have his first accident in an airplane while at Gardner. Fortunately, it was little more than a fender bender. While he was taxiing out to one of the base's runways, his wing struck another airplane. Damage was minor. There was only a cryptic report in his service file, but no reprimand was ever issued by anyone higher up the command ladder.

His last day at Gardner was October 27, 1941. His next stop would be Luke Army Airfield near Phoenix, Arizona, where he would undergo his final advanced pilot training. Hard work and natural ability had paid off. He was accepted as a fighter pilot trainee. Luke would offer still more flat land and dust. But if he was successful there, he would realize his dream of becoming a fighter pilot. And at his next stop after Arizona, he would be working with a real fighter, not a balsa-wood scale model.

With a full week of leave before he was to report to Luke Field, he bought a round-trip ticket on a passenger plane—his first time to fly commercially—hitched a ride down to Los Angeles to catch the flight, and, after multiple stops along the way, eventually landed in Minneapolis. From there, he took a bus through blowing snow up to Poplar to surprise his family. Surprised they were when he showed up in the middle of the night and woke everyone up.

As it happened, with all the travel to and from airports in sour weather, and then the bus ride to Poplar, he got to spend only one full day at home. He had planned to rent one of the yellow Pipers and give young family members a ride, but the weather assured that would not happen. Even so, it was good to see and spend a few precious hours with everyone for the first time since the end of May, five whole months prior. It would be his last time home for much longer than that.

His intent was to fly back to Los Angeles and leave Taft for Phoenix with the other members of his class, as ordered. Once again Mother Nature failed to cooperate. The plane from Minneapolis ended up being grounded by weather in Iowa. Afraid he would not get back to Gardner in time if he waited out the storms, he took a series of train rides until he finally found an airport that was not socked in—in Salt Lake City, Utah—and from there caught a DC-3 on to Los Angeles. Finally, back at Gardner, he got two hours of sleep on his stripped barracks bunk before the bus departed for Phoenix.

At least it was warm there. Warm and sunny. After a week of wet snow, wind, and swirling clouds out the windows of his flights, various buses, trains, and bedroom window back in Poplar, he considered the weather out his military bus window that morning in Arizona to be a good omen. Good flying weather! It was just before seven a.m. on November 4, 1941, when the bus pulled through the main gate at Luke Army Airfield amid the cacti and stretches of moonscapelike desert west of Phoenix.

About the same time that Dick Bong and his class arrived and began to unload, 6,000 miles away, Hirohito, the sacred leader and Emperor of Japan, gave his final go-ahead for an ambitious, long-gestating plan. A plan to stage a surprise aerial bombing attack on the US Navy Pacific Fleet at its home port in Pearl Harbor, on the island of Oahu in Hawaii. Japan's expectation was that the United States, for all its haughty talk and constant warnings aimed at the empire, would never enter a war against Japan—and likely not its fellow Tripartite Pact signees, Germany and Italy—if its naval force in the Pacific was decimated. The West Coast of the United States would be virtually unguarded. Japan could then continue its expansion, displacing what it considered European and American colonialist occupiers all around the Pacific, and stretch the empire south to Indochina, the Philippines, and Australia, and then westward, even as far as the Middle East.

As history would soon reveal, the attack on Pearl Harbor had the opposite result. Instead of pulling in its horns, America responded with a declaration of war against not only Japan but also the Axis powers in Europe. That would be accompanied by an unprecedented ramp-up in manufacturing of war matériel and enlistments of new servicemen. The attack also brought about a strong national resolve that would eventually lead to a hard-won victory. Pearl Harbor awakened a sleeping giant.

That attack would occur just over a month after Dick Bong's unit unpacked their bus in Arizona. One month after Pearl Harbor, he would receive his pilot's wings.

Then the farm boy would play a big role in his country's response to that deadly sneak attack.

CHAPTER FIVE

DIRTY LAUNDRY

General George Churchill Kenney would interact directly with Richard Bong many times over the next three years, far more than with most pilots, and even after Kenney was chosen for the highest Air Forces command position in the Pacific. The first time the two met, Kenney was commander of the Fourth Air Force, based near San Francisco at Hamilton Airfield. The general was not only in charge of air protection up and down the West Coast and 500 miles out into the Pacific Ocean, but he also oversaw all the various training facilities in the region for future pilots of USAAF fighters and bombers.

Kenny's first dealings with Bong came when the young pilot atypically found himself in serious trouble. That came soon after Bong arrived at Hamilton, which he hoped would be his final Stateside billet. The two officers would interact much more when General Kenney later became air commander for the AAF's Southwest Pacific campaigns. Regardless of his role, Kenney was notorious for picking favorites, personally choosing the men he wanted to be flying warplanes for him. He specifically and re- peatedly selected Dick Bong, despite—but also because of—that bit of trouble while they were both stationed at Hamilton.

Kenney would later recall, "Everyone who knew Bong in those days knew that he was a fine, likable youngster belong- ing to a nice, well brought-up, close-knit family. If it had not been for the combination of airplanes and a war, he probably would have been a farmer, and a good one. He didn't smoke or drink. The only times he ever seems to have worried his family were when he got his hands on the steering wheel of a car or a truck."

Unlike many twenty-one-year-olds far from home for the first time, Bong never pushed the limits while on leave, nor did he have any issues whatsoever with fellow trainees or instruc- tors. Though he sometimes took air drills and exercises to the extreme and gave his classmates and instructors some anxious moments, he always knew when to stop pressing before putting anyone in any real danger. He got along with everybody. Unlike so many of his classmates who got roaring drunk or ended up in bar fights to let off steam, Bong preferred spending his precious little bit of idle time singing in the quartet, writing letters home, giving his buddies recitals on the clarinet, and visiting relatives who lived in Southern California.

Of course, he was also proving himself to be an exceptional pilot, trying out other aircraft that came to Luke Field, taking long aerial excursions with fellow trainees as far away as Wichita, doing spectacular loops in the deeper cuts of the Grand Can- yon, and even flying a plane for several scenes of the Hollywood production *Thunder Birds*, which starred Preston Foster and Gene

Tierney. Mostly, though, he followed orders, caused no trouble, and flew his plane better than just about anybody else.

That was why, about two months after Bong reported to Hamilton Airfield, it was a surprise to all when he was called to a meeting with an angry General Kenney. And that he would be accused of serious shenanigans while supposedly on a training mission from his newest base, just across the Golden Gate Bridge from San Francisco.

Before being transferred to Hamilton, Bong had continued to show his ability at Luke Field, impressing all the right people. His commander there, Brigadier General Ennis Whitehead—another man under whom he would one day serve in the Pacific Theater—was quoted as saying, "[Bong] made the best score in the rather limited gunnery training which we conducted on ground targets and on towed targets with AT-6 advanced trainers carrying one .30-caliber machine gun mounted in each wing. Bong could simply fly an AT-6 better than his contemporaries."

The AT-6 was the North American Aviation AT-6, yet another step up in training aircraft from the Piper Cub, the Stearman Kaydet, and the Vultee BT-13 Valiant that Bong had already mastered. The plane had carried many names since its introduction by North American in 1935. The US Navy called it the "SNJ." The British dubbed it the "Harvard." But the popular name for the model used by the US Army Air Forces was "Texan," because it was manufactured in the Lone Star State.

As expected, Bong found the AT-6 to be a much more complex airplane than his previous trainers. That made him happy. The Texan sported retractable landing gear, a bigger and more powerful engine—a Pratt & Whitney nine-cylinder radial engine providing up to 600 horsepower—a variable-pitch propeller, and a hydraulics system. It had a top speed of over 200 miles per hour and a range up to 700 miles. He knew this would be the last step before he finally climbed into the cockpit of whatever fighters he would be flying for real. He intended to make the most of it, and according to General Whitehead's assessment, he certainly did.

He performed so well, in fact, that when he graduated from gunnery school at Luke Field in January of 1942, he was ordered not to a new base but to remain in Arizona. He was going to be a gunnery instructor, right there at Luke Field. Now, that was a big disappointment to him. With the war underway, he most wanted to be flying over Germany or some Japanese-occupied island, striking a blow for his country. But he accepted the development. Such duty would only improve his aim until he was shooting at something other than targets being towed above the Sonoran Desert. Plus, he could show other upcoming pilots how it should be done.

He was so involved in his work that he hardly noticed how quickly time passed. Even before he completed his training and received his pilot wings, he had been planning on going home for Christmas. Obviously, the Japanese attack in Hawaii changed those plans, just as it did for so many millions of others. Like most military facilities on or near the West Coast, Luke Field was locked down for security reasons until January 2, just in case the Japanese launched an attack on the mainland. Leave was hard to come by. Bong did get to see his parents, though, when they came out to attend his graduation ceremonies on January 9. Then, with only a week's worth of free time between completing this phase of training and beginning his instructor role, he decided not to tempt the winter weather gods with a hasty trip back to Wisconsin.

It was during his time as an instructor at Luke that Dick Bong got his first close-up look at the relatively new P-38 fighter. He immediately fell in love with the airplane and hoped that would be his ride once he was in the war. A pilot had flown his Lightning down so he could experiment with the plane's nose-mounted guns. Putting all a fighter's armament in the plane's nose was a true innovation for US aircraft. Guns were usually mounted on the wings on single-engine fighters, away from the propeller. But with the Lightning's two propellers on its wings, it made sense to have the guns placed in the nose of the nacelle, directly in front of the cockpit and pilot.

The Army Air Forces' initial order for thirteen of the Lightnings had been delivered the previous fall. Some early problems with the plane had been addressed. Others lingered. It certainly had a mixed reception and reputation. Some commanders and pilots loved it. Others remained skeptical about the odd duck's performance. Still others were openly afraid of the bird.

Bong was captivated when he got his first up-close look. The airplane was the first in the AAF fleet to make such extensive use of stainless steel and to have a remarkably smooth skin made up of flush-riveted aluminum panels, an innovation developed by Howard Hughes for his H-1 Racer. That reduced drag and made the P-38 that much faster.

There were good reasons for the way the Lightning's guns were configured. With the guns on the wings, trajectories had to be set up for bullets to crisscross at some defined distance ahead of the plane where the target would hopefully be. This problem, termed convergence, meant the pilot had to be more conscious of how far away his target would be when he fired or else the bullets would scatter before they got to what he was aiming for. Nose-mounted guns had no such requirement. That allowed pilots to shoot from a much greater distance, up to a thousand yards in the case of the usual armament on the P-38. And as Bong himself would note in a letter to his parents, all he had to do was aim the airplane, not the guns, at whatever he wanted to hit.

It was inevitable that Bong found himself in the same airspace as the P-38 while it was down there in Arizona. The Lightning pilot would later share with Luke instructor Barry Goldwater his thoughts on the young gunnery instructor.

"[Bong] was a very bright student," Goldwater later wrote. "But the most important thing came from a P-38 check pilot who told me that Bong was the finest natural pilot he ever met. There was no way he could keep Bong from getting on his tail, even though he [Bong] was flying an AT-6 Texan, a very slow airplane."

The recommendations from Whitehead, Goldwater, and others worked. In mid-April, Bong received the orders he had so long coveted. On May 1, 1942, he was to report to Hamilton Army Airfield to begin training in P-38s.

Formally opened in May of 1934, the airfield was originally a bomber facility, but in December of 1940, it had been transitioned to a fighter base primarily hosting P-40 Warhawk squadrons. Then, hastily, on December 7, 1941, it was designated as one of the prime air defense bases for the West Coast. And then, just as abruptly, on January 5, 1942, it became the home of Western Defense Command and the Fourth Air Force, both under the command of General George C. Kenney.

Kenney was already hearing good things about Dick Bong and several other newly minted pilots coming up from Arizona as newly commissioned officers. General Whitehead had written to Kenney, saying he was getting, in Second Lieutenant Richard Bong, one of the hottest pilots he had seen in years. Whitehead noted that the AAF would be hearing about Bong and the others for years. "And so will the Japs!" he promised.

As it happened, neither General Kenney nor the young hotshot pilot would have occasion to interact directly with the other until early July, and that meeting came under inauspicious circumstances. It seemed the entire San Francisco civilian government and local media were up in arms about the recent antics of some of the Fourth Air Force's showboating pilots. The flyboys had been observed doing loops in P-38 fighters around the spires that supported the middle section of the iconic Golden Gate Bridge. Their treacherous antics caused general panic and a massive traffic jam.

Then one reckless scoundrel had flown on into the city, buzzing right up Market Street, seemingly only feet above the pavement, so low he could wave from the cockpit to people occupying the office buildings along one of the city's busiest thoroughfares. Again, traffic was snarled and many observers, fearing it was a Japanese air attack, ran about in a panic, seeking shelter.

Finally, in an especially risky move, the crazy pilot zoomed eastward, off across the bay, almost touching the wave tops along the way, and then buzzed several neighborhoods there. At one point, he flew his fighter so low and fast that he blew one lady's freshly washed laundry right off her clothesline. Then he climbed away and headed north, back to the base, damage done.

It was common knowledge around Hamilton Field that one of the culprits guilty of some of the day's crimes was none other than good old straight-arrow Dick Bong. When General Kenney received a full report along with all the eyewitness accounts, he summoned Bong to his headquarters. There had been pointed instructions from AAF headquarters that all such foolish behavior—and there had been plenty of it around all the bases since training had so dramatically ramped up—was to result in the harshest punishment, including court-martials, and if the offenders were found guilty, they were to be kicked out of the Air Forces into the regular Army—or, in the most egregious cases, sent to military prison.

While Kenney awaited his meeting with the hotshot young pilot, he went ahead and sent word that Bong was to be confined to his barracks. He was to leave only for a day job behind a desk at headquarters. And no flying. The kid was grounded until further notice.

After reviewing the thick report file, Kenney contemplated harsher punishment. It was important to discourage anyone else under his command from engaging in such irresponsible behavior. Sure, the trainees and new pilots were frustrated from all the getting ready. They were anxious to go win the war. But one bad move on their part could be tragic.

When Bong showed up, Kenney was ready to make an example of him. He told his aide to send the young second lieutenant in.

"In walked one of the nicest-looking cherubs you ever saw in your life," Kenney later wrote. "I doubted if he was old enough to shave. He was just a little blond-haired Swedish boy about five feet six, with a round, pink baby face and the bluest, most innocent eyes, now opened wide and a bit scared. Someone must have told him how serious this court-martial thing could be."

Frightened or not, Bong did not try to lie his way out of the mess he was in. He explained that he wanted only to go to war and defend his country as a fighter pilot. He told Kenney he understood that, in a lapse that lasted only a few minutes, he had done some of those foolish things—not all of them—and that he hoped the general would understand and go easy on him.

"He didn't know it yet, but he had already won," Kenney later admitted. But he still made Bong stand at attention while giving him a proper chewing out. He made sure the kid understood that not only had he gotten himself in trouble but that his actions reflected negatively on the Army Air Forces and even on the general himself. Then Kenney let Bong off the hook with a surprising admission.

"Son, the fact is if you did not want to do loops around that bridge or fly down Market Street at second-floor level, I frankly would not want you in my Air Force. But you are not going to do it again, right?"

· Then, as the general ripped up the report in front of him, he told Bong there would still be a price to pay. He was to report the very next Monday morning to the home of the woman in Oakland whose laundry he had blown off her clothesline. There, he was to do any washing she might need done and hang it out on the clothesline to dry. Then he was to do chores for her until the clothes were ready to take back off the line. He would do so, fold them, and put them away wherever she instructed him to.

As a pilot trainee a quarter century earlier, George Kenney had been unable to resist flying under several bridges on New York City's East River on his own initial solo flight. He had received a very similar dressing-down from his commander. He could certainly understand how a twenty-one-year-old kid would feel, flying a fine airplane like the P-38 and wanting to put it through its paces. He knew that Dick Bong had caught the same "fever" Kenney had when he first learned to fly, and he did not blame the youngster at all. He only needed to make certain it never happened again. And that Bong's example might prevent others from doing silly things that could quickly turn deadly.

A duly chastised and grateful Bong had just left Kenney's office when the general's phone rang. It was Hap Arnold, summoning Kenney to Washington, DC, to discuss his new assignment. That would be taking command of the entire Allied air war in the Pacific.

It would be that job that would allow General Kenney's career to once again become entangled with that of the "blond-haired Swedish boy."

CHAPTER SIX

BIDING TIME

To Dick Bong, it sometimes seemed that time was standing still. When he wrote home, he tried to avoid complaining, always putting a positive spin on the news, but he had to gripe just a bit about how long it was taking for him to finally get his orders to go to war. He was not the type to brag, either, but he was convinced he had learned all he could without actually sparring in midair with some guy who was simultaneously trying to blow him out of the sky. Within a week of piloting his first P-38 Lightning, he was surer than ever that he could hold his own against whatever the Japanese, Germans, or Italians might be able to throw at him. Based on his experience, he was sure that the remarkable warplane gave him a decided advantage over whatever the enemy might be flying. Now he just wanted the chance to prove it.

On the other hand, and despite his own impatience, he had to marvel at how fast things were changing, in both the war and the US Army. When he had enlisted in May of 1941, more than a year earlier, there were rumors of war. Common wisdom was the US had no appetite for such an armed conflict. That had changed abruptly, shockingly, the first Sunday in December. Even before then, the branch of service for which he had signed up had undergone a significant reorganization and even a name change. The aircraft he was dreaming of eventually flying had shifted considerably, too. And then, shortly after he was transferred to Hamilton Army Airfield, his commanding officer was suddenly kicked upstairs. That was just after they had met in person and under rather tense circumstances.

Now General Kenney was headed out to the Pacific to oversee the air war against the Japanese Empire. Bong could only hope this development might hasten getting him into action.

The young flier had fallen in love with the fighter plane he was now learning, the one he would, presumably, be taking to battle shortly. He found the P-38 to be much faster than anything he had yet flown, thanks in part to its powerful twin engines. Some pilots were convinced the plane could approach the speed of sound if put into a steep, powered dive, but nobody wanted to try that. Engineers and pilots were convinced the sound barrier would never be broken and attempting to do so was suicidal.

The velocity and nimbleness of the Lightning had already caused accidents, some of them fatal. Even so, it was mostly a stable, smooth-flying, and maneuverable craft. Except, of course, for that nagging high-speed tail flutter issue, which pilots were still managing to work around. When Dick had the chance to practice shooting at targets in his first Lightning, he was thrilled at how well he could line the plane up on a target and kill it. He could do so without considering convergence of the bullets or how far he was from whatever he was shooting at. The canopy on the Lightning also offered him a 360-degree view, and he already knew how valuable that could be in a dogfight. Enemy pilots of all nationalities loved to sneak up behind a target and shoot before the unsuspecting pilot even knew he was being stalked.

Dick had heard that General Kenney was an especially big fan of the P-38 as well. Word was, he had been trying to get as many ordered, built, and in the air in the Pacific as possible. Lockheed was doing the best they could, but Kenney was impatient. He was convinced this plane would make a big difference in a war that was not going well for the Allies.

For security reasons, Bong could not go into details to his family, but he did write home about the P-38. "Woo-hoo! What an airplane! That is all I can say," he raved.

Bong had arrived at Hamilton Army Airfield on May 1, but it would actually be May 12 before he would get to fly one of the Lightnings. More frustration and waiting. Though he had been ready to strap in and crank one up, there was necessarily more class time to familiarize him and others with the differences they would encounter in such a unique fighter plane. Then, to prepare them for piloting the more complex twin-engine aircraft, they'd had to first gain adequate seat time in the Lockheed 12A Electra Junior; designated as the C-40 by the Army, that aircraft had positions up front for a pilot and a copilot/instructor. Only then had they been allowed, after a long list of cautions, to take off in one of the P-38s.

It was only a month later, on June 12, that Bong got carried away while at the stick of his Lightning and got in Dutch with Kenney. (Bong would always maintain that his only crime that day had been buzzing the house of a fellow pilot across the bay, that it had been the three other young pilots who were responsible for the San Francisco mischief. But he had seen no good in arguing with a general.)

That meeting and the dressing-down by the big boss did not happen until three weeks after the crime. That, too, had been an interminably long wait during which Bong would not be allowed to fly. Bong feared he was to be busted and sent to the infantry. Over those long three weeks, he had convinced himself he would never fly an airplane for the Army again.

Though not nearly as bad as what he feared, Dick's punishment hit hard. Not only did he have to help the lady in Oakland with her laundry and grass mowing, but he was also confined to his barracks and grounded from the day after the incident until July 27, a full six weeks. Not being allowed to fly was bad enough, but his confinement to the base led to two other huge disappointments.

First, his mother and sister Nelda had flown out to see him before anyone knew he would be in purgatory by the time they got there. Their timing was terrible. They arrived in San Francisco the day after the incident that led to his confinement. Since he could not leave the barracks, he was at first informed that he would not even be able to visit with them, regardless of how far they had traveled or how long it had been since he had seen them. Then, at the last minute, he got special permission to spend some time with his mother but was not allowed to see his sister at all.

The second setback quite literally changed history. On June 16, word came down that Bong's squadron was to immediately depart Hamilton Army Airfield and be transported to England, there to join the Eighth Air Force and ultimately move south to fight in North Africa and the Mediterranean. Had Dick Bong not been serving his penance, he would have packed up his gear and moved out with his fellow members of the 49th Squadron of the 14th Fighter Group. He would have almost certainly spent the rest of World War II in North Africa and the Mediterranean. There is no doubt he would still have been one of the AAF's top fighter pilots, but it is also likely he would not have been able to tally nearly as many kills or make as big a difference in that war zone as he ultimately did in the Pacific.

For many reasons, fighter-ace status was much more difficult to achieve in the war in Europe than in the Pacific, where Dick Bong would eventually end up. The top US ace in Europe in World War II would be Francis "Gabby" Gabreski with twenty-eight kills, all of them over occupied France and Germany, not North Africa or the Mediterranean. That was twelve fewer than Bong would eventually get.

There was another subplot to the story that would determine where he would ultimately fight for his country. While Bong was briefly visiting with his mother and working away at his desk job penance at the headquarters of the Fourth Air Force at Hamilton Army Airfield, big moves were being made in the upper echelon of the military to try to change the course of the war. Moves that would directly impact the futures of both Dick Bong and General George Kenney. The first sign of this development was the call to Kenney from Hap Arnold the same day as Kenney's come-to-Jesus with Bong.

General Douglas MacArthur, commander of the Southwest Pacific Area, wanted a new commander of Allied Air Forces to serve at his headquarters in Brisbane, Australia. This was to boost the effectiveness of the floundering air war. MacArthur had two choices. One was Brigadier General Jimmy Doolittle, the Medal of Honor recipient who had led the historic first bombing run of the war against the Japanese Home Islands on April 18, 1942, flying bombers off an aircraft carrier. The other choice was General George C. Kenney, the commander of the Fourth Air Force at Hamilton Army Airfield in California and, most recently, Dick Bong's judge and jury.

MacArthur chose Kenney. We can only speculate whether Bong would have gone to the Pacific had MacArthur not made the decision he did.

General Doolittle went on to head air forces first in the Mediterranean, then later in all of Europe. Had Dick Bong been allowed to depart Hamilton with his squadron and be under Doolittle's command, that would likely have been where he spent the war. Meanwhile, Kenney headed west to work with MacArthur in Brisbane. There he would demonstrate his strong preference for the P-38 aircraft and build up a fleet of the odd-duck warplanes as quickly as he could. He would also soon take personal interest in a certain young but gifted P-38 pilot along with some of Bong's cohorts who had also caught his eye.

Bong was back in the cockpit of a Lightning the moment he was freed from his sentence. Though he was now a man without a squad, he technically flew as part of the 84th Fighter Squadron. That group had also just received orders to head for England, but Bong would not make that move, either. Instead, he continued flying various missions out of Oakland Airport, across the bay from San Francisco, where the 84th had been housed. That meant making mostly defensive patrols up and down the California coast, escorting planes or shipping from Hawaii to San Francisco, or ferrying P-38s from one base to another.

The waiting continued throughout August. Although he was flying almost every day, he was not, in his opinion, doing anything useful or important. And nothing to really help win the war. He was hearing things were not going well, especially in the Pacific, despite all the upbeat news on the radio and in the theater newsreels. The US had scored a major victory back in June at the Battle of Midway, but that was one of the few bright spots. The invasion of Guadalcanal in the Solomon Islands had begun the first week of August, but the going there was rough, slow, and deadly. That brutal campaign would not be over and declared a victory for five more months.

As noted, the reason General Kenney was now in Brisbane and part of MacArthur's staff was because the Allies in the Pacific were having an especially difficult time with the air war against the empire. Japan had aircraft at least equal to those in the US fleet, and the well-trained, brutally dogged Japanese pilots had had a head start.

When General Kenney arrived at his new job in Australia, he

was met with discouraging reports from his commanders in the field. Not a single squadron for which he would be responsible was operating at more than half strength, woefully short of both pilots and airplanes. Parts, engines, ammunition, bombs, and especially gasoline were in short supply, with rarely more than three days' worth available. Even food and other basic supplies were severely lacking. Kenney had himself a real problem. He figured one way to solve it was with better airplanes and talented pilots who knew how to fly them.

Dick Bong kept his bag packed, sitting ready for the day when he would finally receive orders. Bong knew that General Kenney liked him. That Kenney wanted and needed pilots like Bong to put into those P-38s he was desperately trying to get delivered out there. That was what it would take to start making some headway against the Japanese Zeros, other Mitsubishis, and Nakajimas.

But as August sluggishly rolled over into September, Dick was beginning to think that Kenney had forgotten about him. Or maybe had thought more about the crimes the young pilot had been accused of and decided he really did not need that kind of troublemaker on his team.

There was nothing Bong could do, though. Nothing but learn the Lightning inside and out, fly her hard when he was over sparsely populated territory or the vast Pacific and in no danger of being accused of hot-rodding or buzzing. He pushed her to see how she would respond and practiced shooting those nose-mounted guns at targets at every opportunity. Otherwise, all he could do was wait.

Which was exactly what he did.

CHAPTER SEVEN

ACE OF ACES

As part of his efforts to turn around the air war in the South Pacific, General Kenney formed the 9th Fighter Squadron—the "Flying Knights"—of the 49th Fighter Group of the Fifth Air Force. It was to be an all–P-38 unit. He had to wait to send the new group into battle until he had enough P-38s and the men he knew could fly them. According to the general, one of the keys was to handpick many of the newer pilots and pull the strings necessary to have them sent his way. The ones he coveted were the recently graduated airmen who had caught the eye of their commanders at the bases where they had done their final training. Special pilots who had shown above-average skill and demonstrated the aggressiveness it would take to prevail against the Japanese.

Kenney already had several in mind. No, he had not forgotten the short, cherub-faced Dick Bong. He specifically requested that Hap Arnold assign the youngster to him. Arnold kindly obliged.

Those orders came on September 1, 1942, and Bong was off early the very next morning on the longest airplane ride of his young life. Brisbane, Australia, on the big island's eastern coast north of Sydney, was just over 7,000 miles from San Francisco. He and several other newly assigned pilots were aboard a Consolidated Air LB-30, a transport variant of the B-24 long-range bomber. It took them just over a week of stops and starts to finally land near Brisbane on September 9.

The first thing the group of P-38 jockeys learned upon reporting for duty was that their squadron did not yet have any Lightnings for them to fly. The primary aircraft employed against the Japanese at the time was the Curtiss-Wright P-40 Warhawk. Like some others, this was a plane whose capabilities were not fully appreciated during the war. But it was certainly the best available. The Warhawk was a good fighter and ground-attack warplane; more than two hundred Allied pilots in Europe and the Pacific earned ace status in P-40s. It helped that they were relatively quick and cheap to build and very durable, cutting maintenance requirements. However, they did not perform well at high altitudes, and that was where the Japanese planes were proving to be a much more serious threat, especially against Allied bombers. Kenney was adamant that the P-38s would finally be able to match or exceed the empire's equipment, and with the right boys flying them, they could turn the course of the air war.

So it was that Bong and his fellow passengers on the LB-30 found that even after all that training and waiting and traveling and waiting some more, they would have to cool their heels just a bit longer, until some P-38s showed up. That was expected to be in about the first week of October. To keep the pilots sharp, they would take turns flying the few Lightnings available to them, but that would amount to only about five or six hours per week of total seat time each.

As it turned out, it would be the middle of November before Bong climbed into the cockpit of the brand-new P-38 assigned to him and gave it a checkout run. As with the previous Lightnings he had piloted back in the States, this one felt like a natural extension of his own limbs and brain. He swore the airplane could anticipate his commands and start its maneuvers before he even manipulated the stick, throttle, or pedals.

Then, on November 15, 1942, he headed out for a spot that would—unbeknownst to him at the time—become his home base for the next year plus some. That was Fourteen-Mile Field—also known as Schwimmer Field, its official name—just outside the city of Port Moresby on the southeastern coast of the massive island of New Guinea. This rugged tropical island, very near the equator, was only about ninety miles north of the Australian coast, across the Torres Strait, but centuries behind its southern neighbor in development and civilization. Early in the war, it had become an unlikely but key strategic location for both the Japanese Empire and the Allies.

For several years before and then immediately after the entry of the United States into the war, the Japanese had swiftly swept through and captured many of the islands in the western and southwestern Pacific, claiming, among others, important places like the Philippines, Guam, Tinian and the rest of the Marianas, New Britain, the Solomon Islands—especially Guadalcanal—and most of New Guinea. From there, it seemed inevitable that they would cut off and neutralize Australia, eventually capturing that vast nation. It was in this area that the Allies decided they had to make a stand, to protect Australia and stop the southward advance by the enemy and then, if that strategy was successful, begin to push back, to hack away at the southernmost extent of the Empire of Japan and shove them back toward their Home Islands.

There was disagreement about the best route for that push-back. General Douglas MacArthur preferred island-hopping along a southern route, even bypassing some enemy-held islands, with the goal of recapturing the Philippines. That would fulfill his promise of "I shall return," famously made in March of 1942 when he and his family and staff hastily evacuated ahead of the Japanese invasion. The US Navy and Admiral Chester Nimitz, Commander in Chief, Pacific Ocean Areas, preferred a more northern strategy, with his goal being to capture the island of Formosa, now Taiwan. From there, he felt they could cut off the shipment of natural resources from Borneo, Malaysia, and the Philippines to the Japanese Home Islands. They could also stop the vital movement by sea of troops, supplies, and ammunition to that region. Nimitz believed Formosa would offer not only the best place to launch saturation-bombing missions against the Home Islands but also the perfect staging area for the inevitable Allied invasion of Japan.

On a couple of points the two commanders agreed. To win the war, the empire's thrust would first have to be stopped in the area of the Coral Sea, the Solomon Sea, and the Bismarck Sea and on islands like New Guinea and New Britain. The US Army and Navy also agreed they needed to capture territory close enough to begin regular and effective bombing of the Japanese Home Islands. General Doolittle had proven that flying bombers off aircraft carriers bound for Japan was possible but not even remotely practical. The Allies would have to go through or around enemy-held islands to ultimately secure places from which to launch and reliably retrieve bombers.

In May of 1942, both sides still held territory on New Guinea, but the Allies knew Japan intended to control it all, especially the southeastern portion from which an assault on Australia could be launched. Intercepted enemy naval messages confirmed that a Japanese invasion force was on its way to capture the last portion of the island still held by the Allies: New Guinea's only major city, Port Moresby. That invasion force was intercepted and turned away in a key skirmish in the Battle of the Coral Sea. Though historians typically call that battle a draw, repelling the enemy force bound for Port Moresby was the first instance in which the Japanese advance in the Pacific was stymied. And the empire's aircraft carriers that were damaged in the Coral Sea in history's first all-aircraft-carrier battle had to be sent back to Tokyo Bay for repairs. That made them unavailable to the Japanese at the Battle of Midway a month later, a major factor in the US victory there.

Early in 1942, Japan had begun constructing and manning a huge base at Rabaul, on the recently taken island of New Britain, just northeast of New Guinea. Then air bases popped up all around the region. Japan believed air dominance would lead to control of the seas and ensure the empire would one day extend all the way to the south coast of Australia. That led to New Guinea and the surrounding area becoming the epicenter of battles to control the skies for much of the first two years of the war.

This despite the huge island appearing to be hardly worth fighting for. Most of its land is choked with impossibly thick tropical forest. A rugged, tall mountain chain, the Stanley Mountains, bisects the island. There are few roads, even to this day. And many of its inhabitants remain primitive with some still practicing headhunting. Still, both sides in the war recognized the strategic importance of New Guinea, even if it did seem stuck in the Stone Age.

The Japanese had established a major air base at Lae on the island's northeastern coast. There were many more airstrips scraped from jungle at other spots. That made Fourteen-Mile Field and other airfields constructed by the US Army Air Forces near Port Moresby critically and tactically important. That was why General Kenney sent every P-38 and fighter pilot he could get up there. Their job was to begin claiming the skies for the Allies.

It was also why General Ennis "Whitey" Whitehead was dispatched from Arizona to Fourteen-Mile Field. His job was straightforward. Use that crucial air base in tenuous territory with mostly unproven planes and pilots to turn around the war in the Southwest Pacific. Yes, the man with such a tough job was the same General Whitehead who had been Dick Bong's commander while the kid was training at Luke Field in Arizona. The same commander who had taken time to write to General Kenney, bragging on the young pilot from Wisconsin who would soon pass through Kenny's command at Hamilton Army Airfield on San Francisco Bay.

Kenney and others—including MacArthur—understood that the nature of warfare had changed significantly since the "War to End All Wars" in Europe more than two decades prior. That conflict had first demonstrated the value of airpower. Now any nation that could not control the skies had little chance of winning a war. Carrier-based warplanes were certainly a crucial part of that. For the first time in history, a landing field could be moved to waters much closer to where the targets were. The Battle of the Coral Sea and the Battle of Midway had further proven the point, but the surprise Japanese attack on Pearl Harbor had been the true wake-up call. The empire's aircraft carriers had made that attack possible.

Despite the value of the "flattops," the Army's land-based aircraft would need to play a role in achieving air superiority. Carrier-based planes were limited by fuel and design. The aircraft flying off the decks of those big ships had to be able to land and take off on what amounted to very short runways. They also needed wings that could be folded up for storage. Land-based aircraft had no such limitations. As good a warplane as the P-38 was, it would never have been practical to fly it off aircraft carriers.

As the newly arrived squadron at Port Moresby was busy getting ready to go to war, they were blessed with a visit by one of their true heroes. Of course, Eddie Vernon Rickenbacker was a hero to most of a generation of Americans for what he had accomplished in World War I. The aviator—a former race car driver and mechanic—had been that war's top American ace fighter pilot. That was a record many believed would stand forever. Rickenbacker was also awarded the Medal of Honor and is still generally considered to be America's most highly decorated flier.

In October of 1942, Secretary of War Henry Stimson saw the need for morale building among the USAAF personnel in the Pacific and Europe. He also wanted an expert's opinion on how things were going out there. Stimson asked Rickenbacker to go visit units in both theaters of operation. He also wanted the hero to give his opinion on how the air war was being conducted and make any recommendations he thought appropriate. Rickenbacker jumped at the chance, even though the trip would once again put him in harm's way.

Fast Eddie, the founder and chief executive of Eastern Airlines, was still recovering from a near-fatal crash of one of his own company's flights near Atlanta, Georgia, in February 1941. Newspapers initially reported he had died in the accident And now he was perfectly willing to climb aboard military planes and head off for long and treacherous flights to various hot war zones in service to his nation.

His visit to Europe went well. Then, in late October, bound for Canton Island and then on to Australia, the B-17 aircraft in which he was flying strayed off course, ran out of fuel, and crashed into the sea. Rickenbacker survived, but he and the other crew members found themselves adrift without food and water— other than what little rain they could catch—for twenty-four days before ultimately being rescued. But not before the news media once again prematurely proclaimed the death of one of America's true heroes.

Rather than go back home to recover, Rickenbacker flew on

to Australia and then to Port Moresby. As General Kenney would later write, "As soon as he found out the war was in New Guinea, not Australia, that was where he wanted to go." Rickenbacker enjoyed Thanksgiving dinner with General MacArthur and General Kenney in Port Moresby on November 26.

That same day, he toured other USAAF airfields in the area with Kenney, including Fourteen-Mile Field. There he shook hands and spent considerable time with Dick Bong and his fellow pilots, listening to accounts of their very limited exploits so far and what they felt could make things go better. Shortages of planes, parts, fuel, and food were their primary complaints. Rickenbacker confirmed that a big part of the problem was that the European Theater had priority with the USAAF. The troops there had the first choice of most any airplane when it came off the assembly line. General Kenney could only nod knowingly as he listened to Rickenbacker's assessment.

When the subject came up of how many kills Rickenbacker had achieved, Kenney pointed out that the ace had gotten his record twenty-six kills in just over half a year, from April to November in 1918. Rickenbacker modestly noted, "You have to remember that the Germans were pretty thick on the front in those days. We had plenty of targets to shoot at."

Kenney later recalled that it was the typically quiet and reserved Dick Bong, who had said little so far during the discussion, who piped up with a cogent observation.

"Captain Rickenbacker, the Japanese are pretty thick over here, too," he offered.

As the group laughed, General Kenney had a sudden thought.

"Tell you what, Eddie," he said. "I'm going to give a case of the best Scotch whisky to the first one to beat your old record."

Rickenbacker, still pale and skinny from his ordeal in the Pacific Ocean, grinned and quickly added, "Put me down for another case!"

At that time, both men likely felt they would never have to pay off on their offer. Most of the pilots in the group that day had zero kills. And still no airplanes to go out and get any.

The top American pilot at that point, almost a full year into the Pacific War, was Captain Boyd "Buzz" Wagner with eight verified enemy planes shot down. Wagner got the first four in his P-40 Warhawk during action in the Philippines on December 12, 1941, only four days after the Japanese attacked that island nation. Five days later, Wagner engaged in a vicious dogfight before shooting down an enemy Zero, thus claiming his fifth kill and becoming the first verified AAF ace of World War II. He got his other three Zeros while flying for the 8th Fighter Group in New Guinea.

After that, Wagner was sent back to the States—against his wishes—for what his commanders considered to be more vital duty. He was assigned to help develop better training methods for young pilots, employing skills he had picked up in the real world. And he was to spend time with the Curtiss-Wright Corporation to improve the combat capabilities of the Warhawk.

However, only three days after Rickenbacker's Thanksgiving Day visit with Dick Bong and the other pilots at Port Moresby, Buzz Wagner was killed back in the States in a mysterious crash of a P-40. He was flying from Eglin Field on the Florida Gulf

Coast on a short hop up to Maxwell Field at Montgomery, Alabama. His plane and remains were not found until six weeks later, in a pine thicket twenty-five miles east of Eglin Field. The cause of the crash was never revealed.

Kenney and Rickenbacker had no idea the offers of alcohol bounties to the young pilots would stir up such controversy throughout the chain of command. General MacArthur was all for the idea. He even suggested they add a case of champagne for kill number twenty-seven. But others among and outside the military felt it inappropriate to incentivize fighting boys with booze. And though both men General Kenney and Rickenbacker, America's ace of aces—continued to hear about it from all quarters, they simply shrugged it off. Should a pilot be responsible for putting twenty-seven enemy planes into the jungle or the sea, he deserved the Scotch. And so very much more.

"The kids all thought it was a wonderful idea," Kenney wrote. "It wasn't going to make them try any harder than they already were, of course, but it added a bit of levity to the conversation and helped take some of the grim seriousness out of the business of fighting a tough war under primitive conditions in a miserable climate against a skilled and ruthless opponent."

Still, Kenney saw it as a moot point. He later confirmed he did not expect the record to be broken. And he certainly would not have anticipated that the prize would ultimately go to a fresh-faced young farmer from Wisconsin who rarely took a drink.

CHAPTER EIGHT

FIRST TWO

There was about to be still more frustration for the exasperated P-38 jockeys. Despite having a goodly number of the birds finally being delivered to New Guinea, some as early as September, the USAAF experienced a maddening series of delays associated with the newly constructed planes. Something about the climate caused pesky leaks in their cooling systems. When the planes were flying at lower altitudes, the temperature in the cockpit of the Lightning could become almost unbearably hot. Opening the canopy to get some air was not an option. That led to buffeting or shaking of the aircraft. So far, there had been no easy solution for this problem, so the pilots simply learned to live with it in various ways, including spending as little time as necessary at low altitudes. Also, the bulletproof, self-resealing fuel tanks built into the airplane's wings were showing up in New Guinea with big gaps in their welded seams. There was no way to fix them, so Bong and the others had to wait for a new shipment from the manufacturer in the US. This was not uncommon. With assembly lines everywhere in the States running at full capacity to meet the needs of the war effort, quality control often suffered. Then, when the new tanks were delivered, mechanics found they would have to practically rebuild the wings on the '38s to make them fit.

While Bong and his fellow fighter pilots continued to make patrols that were disappointingly limited and fruitless. None of them was enthusiastic about taking on the Japanese and their impressive airplanes while their own machines were not yet in top form. The best known of the Japanese warplanes—and easily one of the best fighter planes in anyone's air force—was the Mitsubishi A6M, named the "Zeke" by the US Air Forces but almost always referred to as the "Zero." ("Zero" came from the last digit of the year in which the aircraft was to be delivered and put into service. In this case, the year was not necessarily 1940. It was for the Japanese year 2600, which also just happened to justify the "0.")

The Zero had already proven itself in China and then in the attacks on Pearl Harbor and the Philippines. US military intelligence had been aware of the plane before the assaults on American soil because of its use in the Chinese invasion, but observers were shocked at how spectacularly well they performed on December 7 directly in front of so many knowledgeable experts. The plane had continued to dominate the P-40 Warhawks and other Allied fighters in action in the year since. And the Japanese also had other aircraft, several of which were only slightly behind the Zero in performance. That included the Nakajima Ki-43 "Oscar," which resembled the Zero so closely that official engagement reports often listed planes shot down as a "Zero or

Oscar." Most pilots did not think it really mattered which one had gone down so long as it had the Japanese red-dot logo on its fuselage and wings.

By mid-December of 1942, enough Lightnings were serviceable to begin using them to fly top cover for bombing missions against Japanese installations at Buna, Gona, Dobodura, and Sanananda, along New Guinea's northern coast. Though these were primitive native villages with rough airstrips, they were also beachheads for troop landings. And they were key positions, already being used to put ashore enemy soldiers as part of a planned march across the island and an eventual assault by land on Port Moresby. US and Australian troops were already fighting the new forces along the shoreline and the choking jungle there.

Though little known today, the Battle of Buna–Gona—as it has been called—was nowhere near the largest but was one of the most vicious of the war. There were heavy losses on both sides and often hand-to-hand clashes were fought under unimaginably horrid conditions. Food and other supplies were hard to come by for both sides. The Allies depended on air cargo drops from Port Moresby and Australia. American aircraft were effective in preventing enemy resupply ships and planes from Rabaul from reaching the remote airstrips and beachheads. There were even widespread reports of Japanese cannibalism of dead troops from both sides.

But General MacArthur was pushing especially hard for his soldiers there to complete the battle and drive the enemy troops back across the Solomon Sea to New Britain. Controlling the north shore of New Guinea was a key goal in the general's plan to eventually move across the front edge of Japanese-held territory—some of which was not as well supplied or defended—and then on to the Philippines. That meant bombers were in the air, escorted by the newly improved P-38s, with Dick Bong flying one of them, for five straight days in late December, including Christmas Day. The mission was to chase away the Japanese troops, establish air bases, and, from there, begin the Allied move west. At least, Bong was getting what he wanted: flying combat missions over enemy territory. But for the five days leading up to December 25, he still had met no enemy fighters to deflect and no Zeros with which to skirmish, and the missions were boringly routine.

Routine until his final trip on Christmas Day. That was when he got his brand-new P-38 shot and wounded. Even then he had no idea that he had taken enemy fire until he set down back at the base and the mechanics began the usual post-mission inspection of his aircraft. They found a bullet hole in the skin of one of the plane's fuselages. It had almost certainly been ground fire. Bong had seen no enemy aircraft. The bullet had done no real damage, but for the first time, Bong felt that he was in the war. People were shooting at him with the intent of killing him. He told fellow pilots that he only wished he could have shot at something or somebody to let them know they were attacking the wrong guy.

Christmas in the remote tropics came and went with no snow, no jingling sleigh bells, no real tree, and no presents from his family. His brother would later write that Dick's mother had sent him a homemade fruitcake, made from a family recipe from the old country. Christmas came and went but no cake arrived at Port Moresby, New Guinea.

Dora had baked, carefully wrapped, and then mailed the fruitcake from Poplar way back in early October, certain she was giving it plenty of time to reach New Guinea so her son and his buddies could enjoy it for the holiday. Mail from the States to that near-inaccessible part of the planet was notoriously unreliable. Sometimes a letter took only a week to make the trek. Sometimes it was months in transit. The promised fruitcake finally showed up in July. July of 1943. Knowing the nature of the confection, Bong was confident it would still be fine to eat. And he did eat it, happily sharing it with his grateful buddies, but a full six months after he had intended to.

Inevitably, Dick Bong and his squadron got their first taste of air-to-air combat. It came on December 27. He was part of a four-plane patrol led by Captain Tommy Lynch, who would later become the commander of the 39th Fighter Squadron and a true challenger to Bong for the most kills in combat. By the twenty-seventh, Lynch already had three confirmed kills in the war, those while flying a Bell P-39 Airacobra fighter, another of the limited-capability aircraft the US had available when the war started.

On the twenty-seventh, Bong was flying as Lynch's wingman. As theirs and the other two P-38s in the squad routinely flew along the northern coast of New Guinea near Buna, they could not have anticipated the action they would see this day. Tommy Lynch would shoot down two more enemy planes to officially qualify as an ace fighter pilot. And Second Lieutenant Richard Bong would tally his first two kills on the way to forty.

In the typical confusion of war, it was never clear where word originated that an imposing force of enemy bombers had been detected. Nor was the Japanese force's intended target ever confirmed. In any case, "coast watchers"—a clandestine group of mostly Australian insurgents who collected intelligence for the Allies throughout the region—were credited by some with initially spotting and reporting the bombers. Some assumed the enemy planes were aiming for Buna and Dobodura. General Kenney would recall that the Japanese force first showed up on radar and was almost certainly on the way to pound Port Moresby and nearby airfields, including Fourteen-Mile, now that those facilities were active and threatening.

Based on that information, eight more P-38s were sent up from Fourteen-Mile Field. They were to meet up with and assist Lynch's group as they intercepted the attackers somewhere over the Stanley Mountains, well before they got to Port Moresby.

It took the newly scrambled group of Lightnings only about twenty minutes to rendezvous with Bong and Lynch at an altitude of 18,000 feet over the tiny grass-hut village of Dobodura, on New Guinea's northern beaches. That was about 125 miles from where they took off. The speed of the P-38 was already paying dividends. They spotted the Japanese bombers and fighter escorts with the help a radio heads-up from some P-40s flying south back to Port Moresby. The Warhawks were escorting a group of cargo planes at 7,000 feet and spied the enemy group high above them. The enemy planes would soon be bombing tired and miserable Allied troops who were slogging through the mud and muck below. Bong, Lynch, and the others were bound to use their new warplanes to assure that never happened.

Once the enemy bomber force was located, nobody took time to get an accurate count of how many there were. Maybe two dozen escort fighters and dive-bombers flying tight formation. To Dick Bong, it must have looked like a flock of geese heading south across Lake Superior from the Canadian prairies. Later, engagement reports by the various pilots would vary in specifics, but it was likely a typical mix for a bomber attack. Some were Zeros. Others were Oscars. The dive-bombers were Aichi D3As, dubbed "Vals" by the AAF. They were another quite competent and fearsome Japanese warplane. Vals, typically flying off aircraft carriers, had inflicted considerable damage at Pearl Harbor and in most engagements since the start of the war. They were certainly capable of taking a toll on the infantry troops dug in around the battlegrounds directly below. Without help, there was not much those soldiers could do about it but duck and pray.

As wingmen are trained to do, Dick Bong flew alongside Tommy Lynch, serving as his eyes as he directed the squad and maneuvered his pilots for an attack position on the Japanese planes. They approached the enemy directly from the blinding glare of a brilliant tropical sun. Hopefully, that would keep them from being seen until they were within close range, ready to announce their presence by opening fire. Once the shooting started, though, it would be every man for himself, though members of the squad would use short shouts on the radio to let teammates know if a Zero was on their tails or approaching from angles that kept them from being seen by other pilots.

When the group opened fire on the top-cover escorts, Dick Bong was able to get off only a short burst of fire on a Zero that had buzzed in from nowhere, lining up on Lynch's tail. Dick could only give Lynch a warning before having to deal with his own problem: suddenly being chased by yet another Zero. One with obvious bad intentions. Dick's first thought was to continue to shoot at Lynch's attacker and protect his friend, but then he saw that his squad leader had made an amazing move, sliding sideways to avoid his attacker, then going into a bank and dive. Lynch would soon be in position to shoot the Zero himself.

Bong instinctively banked hard and made a sharp dive away from his own attacker. He wished he could have seen the look on the Japanese pilot's face when the Lightning simply broke off at an impossibly crisp angle, heading straight down. The move caused breathtaking gravity forces on Bong, but it allowed him to effectively fly away from one of the empire's best. It was almost certainly a shock to him when the Japanese pilot realized that this sleek, odd-looking airplane he had drawn a bead on did not perform like a Warhawk or an Airacobra.

Running away was not Bong's goal. He had to get back into the skirmish as quickly as he could and inflict some serious damage while protecting his guys. He pulled out of the dive just above a stand of palm trees along the shoreline and began a steep climb toward the sun. The P-38's engines screamed with effort but obeyed his commands on the throttle.

Now, though, there was no sign of the Zero he had dived to avoid. But no worries. The sky was thick with dueling aircraft.

That included a perfect target flying along right there in front of him as if waiting for Bong to get back to altitude and shoot him. The Vals had a major flaw: They had fixed landing gear that prevented them from being able to quickly maneuver, to dodge, to divert, to do anything in a big hurry. As Bong pulled out of the climb, this Aichi seemed to be standing still compared to all the other darting and dashing aircraft chasing and firing at one another all over the brightly lit afternoon sky.

Bong forced himself to repeat from muscle memory all those practice approaches on towed targets he had executed high above dusty desert landscapes. Aim the airplane. The guns were right there in front of his cockpit. Get close but not too close. Fire at precisely the right moment.

That was exactly what he did, mostly by instinct. Not too much thinking. Not too much getting ready. Do what came on impulse.

And sure enough, with only a short blast from his nose gun, bits, pieces, and then large chunks of the enemy dive-bomber flew away from the craft as it began to come apart. They rattled against the skin of Bong's Lightning as he flew right through the flotsam he had set loose from the Val. Then flames erupted from several places on what remained of the doomed aircraft as it began a series of rapid death rolls, no longer airworthy. It was ripped apart by gravity and its own momentum all the way down.

Bong watched the Val plummeting, but just long enough to be certain his first target would never fly for the empire again, never drop a bomb on an American soldier or ship. And to make sure that his onboard film camera captured the evidence of his first enemy plane shot down.

But there were still other targets. He had no time to savor or celebrate the accomplishment, the result of all that waiting and getting ready.

Victim number two was suddenly directly in front of him, as if dangling like a gift on a Christmas tree.

It was a Zero. Or at least he thought it was. Not much time to make the determination. It was absolutely an enemy aircraft. And the guy flying the thing had unknowingly turned broadside to him. He was ahead of Bong, straight off the nose of the Lightning's nacelle and well within range. It was so easy a shot, Bong would later remark that he was not sure he deserved credit for this one. Though it was certainly not the case—the pilot was simply occupied with all the other bogeys out there and had not seen Bong and his Lightning—it was as if the Japanese pilot were asking to be shot.

Again, with minimal ammunition expended, Bong quickly had the enemy plane immersed in billowing flames, plunging toward the thick canopy of the jungle far below. The fire he set off was no surprise. Bong knew that as fine a warplane as the Zero was, it had a couple of shortcomings of its own. Ones he and his fellow pilots were more than willing to exploit when given the chance.

The Japanese military and the engineers at Mitsubishi had made one crucial decision in developing the fighter. To make it quicker and more maneuverable in combat than anything flown by any other nation at the time, they constructed the Zeros with no armor plating at all. Only sheet metal and Plexiglas stood between the pilot in the cockpit and enemy bullets. Also, in the rush to get the planes into war, they had decided to forgo developing and installing self-sealing fuel tanks, as the US and other nations had done. If the Zeros' tanks were punctured by gunfire, fuel leaked from them in torrents. If that happened, the gas often found a spark and caught fire. There was no way for the pilot to extinguish it.

Bong did not see a parachute exit the target. He—and his on-board film camera—did see the Zero hit the ground in a gush of flame and black smoke.

Meanwhile, the battle went on all around him, knights engaged in life-and-death jousting amid peaceful, wispy clouds, the radio continually squawking with shouts of ecstatic accomplishment, high-pitched warnings, and enthusiastic attaboys.

Bong soon picked out from the melee a third objective, another Zero that had inadvertently flown directly across his line of sight. It was not nearly so easy a target, though. The pilot of this one had obviously given up and was skedaddling, hoping to live to fight another day. Bong took off, giving chase, and even shot at the guy. Shot far more than he thought he should have had to. But the enemy pilot was good, ducking every round as he climbed and dived, skewed and swerved, trying to shake the American in the odd-looking airplane. Near the end of the pursuit, Bong thought he might have hit and damaged the Mitsubishi, but then he lost him in the clouds and smoke. Since neither he nor his camera could see the plane come apart, catch fire, or crash, he could not claim credit for finishing him off.

So be it. Scoring shoot-downs was a goal. It was not the main goal. Winning the war—that was what he was up here above this unforgiving jungle to do.

He had also been distracted about then by another Val that abruptly came into view, heading away from him, also obviously trying to escape this deadly swarm of P-38s. Bong climbed to the dive-bomber's level, gave chase, and fired several times, but before he could get close enough to have a better shot at the low-profile target of the Val's tail, he realized he was out of ammo. None of the other squad members were coming after him to take up the pursuit. They were all either otherwise engaged or as devoid of firepower as he now was. But the fact was, the enemy pilots had mostly deserted the area by then.

With no means to bring the plane down, he would have to break off the chase.

By their best count, Bong, Lynch, and the others had shot down a dozen—about half—of the bomber force. As noted, Lynch got two of the Oscars, earning ace status. Bong got his first two confirmed kills. One other pilot also claimed two. Best of all, not a single P-38 was lost. And the Americans and their Lightnings had shown the Japanese that things had changed. They now had a formidable new challenge for superiority in the skies over this ugly but strategically crucial part of the planet.

General Kenney was so proud of the group that he left his headquarters, jumped into a jeep, and raced over to Fourteen-Mile Field to personally greet and congratulate the crew as they triumphantly set back down. He made a point of shaking every man's hand as he climbed down from his cockpit. He thanked the support crews, too—the ones who had worked so hard to make the Lightnings as lethal as they were. Then he remained there at the airstrip, despite the pressing business that he had waiting for him back at HQ. That was because he wanted to hear every pilot's story. In detail.

He had also brought along three bottles of celebratory Scotch, a gift from one of the aircraft manufacturers, to share with his "boys." Dick Bong, who rarely took a drink, would confess in a letter home that he politely accepted and finished off a glass of the stuff, but that it was heavily diluted with club soda.

It was, after all, the first time the specific airplane Kenney had lobbied for, the very weapon he wanted to throw at the enemy, and the handpicked twentysomething-year-olds he coveted to fly them had finally been put to the test. A test over hostile territory against the best the Empire of Japan had to offer. And they had passed magnificently. Kenney knew not all encounters would turn out so well. The Japanese would find ways to counter the advantages of the P-38s. They would certainly learn new tactics to thwart the skills and bravado of his own young pilots.

But his theories had been tested. And they had worked.

Kenney would later note that he was so interested in every detail of the December 27 clash that, once they were available, he sat down and read every word of the pilots' post-action reports. He wanted to pick up any nuance or tidbit that might make the next encounter just as positive.

The first thing he noticed about those reports was how detailed and enthusiastic most of them were. The youthful pilots seemed determined to share every element of the action: how their airplanes had performed and how they themselves had conducted the battle in the skies over Dobodura. Although such boisterous reportage did not bother the general at all, most of them, with the typical exuberance of youth, came across as blatantly self-serving, braggadocious, and downright cocky, as if the writers had just won the war almost single-handedly.

However, one of the post-action wrap-ups was decidedly different from all the others. And along with Tommy Lynch's observations, this was the one Kenney most wanted to read. That was the engagement report from Dick Bong, nemesis of bridges, thoroughfares, and wet laundry.

It turned out to be sparse in detail and totally lacking in anything resembling boasting. It was only a few handwritten lines recounting the time he had lifted off from Fourteen-Mile, the time his quartet of planes had rendezvoused with the other eight P-38s over the northern New Guinea coastline, and his altitude at the time, 18,000 feet. Then, with no embellishment at all, he wrote that he had shot down a fighter, believed to be a Mitsubishi Zero, and a bomber, an Aichi Val. The account ended with the time Bong's plane touched down back at Fourteen-Mile Field.

Kenney could only shake his head and smile. This kid from Wisconsin was a different kind of cat!

CHAPTER NINE

"THE SWEDE" STARTS TO WORK

After studying the reports of his P-38 squad's first real encounter with the enemy, General George Kenney arrived at several significant and helpful determinations. Yes, he was proud of his boys and how they had made use of the remarkable capabilities of his preferred warplane. But he also recognized that they had made about every mistake in the book in the process. They were fortunate to have done so much damage up there and still have been able to go home to celebrate.

In their excitement in finally being able to engage the enemy, they had typically fired on the Zeros and Oscars much too early and from too far away. They had also, in many cases, tried to outmaneuver the Japanese pilots, not necessarily using the Lightning's speed and climbing ability to counter typical enemy tactics. The general had been a young pilot once, too. He understood how the new pilots felt, whether while buzzing one another in training or ignoring what they had learned once they were in the heat and frenzy of the fight.

Kenney waited until the squad's post-engagement excitement

had waned a bit, and while admittedly forcing some appearance of being angry with the "kids," he made a point of briefing them so the next encounter might turn out even better. He did not want to dampen their enthusiasm. After all, most of them had trained hard and waited a long time to finally go out and help win the war. But he knew the next dogfight could turn out differently.

Later, in talking with the squad's direct commander, General Whitehead, Kenney shared his concerns but also his opinions about the various men involved in the melee over Dobodura. Whitehead was convinced Tommy Lynch, the Army Air Forces' newest ace, was the best fighter pilot of the group. Kenney agreed that Lynch was not only a fine pilot but also a great leader. But he also believed Lynch sometimes pushed himself too hard. He might quickly burn out.

Whitehead saw his boss's point. But for the time being he needed Lynch up there leading P-38s against the enemy now that the squadron finally had aircraft and pilots to drive them.

"Watch that boy Bong," Kenney then told Whitehead. "There is your top ace of aces in this war. He's just started to work."

General Kenney did have one reservation about Dick Bong and his chances of fulfilling that lofty prediction. And it had nothing to do with Bong's alleged impetuous street-and-bridge buzzing back in San Francisco. Kenney would later write, "If Dick ever realized that he was shooting people instead of clay pigeons, I believed that I would have to pull him out of combat. He was a nice kid, and I hated to think that someday he might hurt an awful lot when he found out what a dirty business war was."

However, it would be just over a week into the new year—1943—when Dick Bong again confirmed the general's confidence in his piloting skills. On January 8, that "cool little Scandinavian boy"—as Kenney often called Bong—officially became an ace fighter pilot.

To continue their air dominance over not only New Guinea but also the entire southern Pacific region, the Japanese had continued to build and reinforce an air base at Lae, a northern-coast town they had initially captured in March of 1942. It was strategically located on Huon Gulf, which faced the Solomon Sea to the east. Lae was usefully close to the major empire stronghold at Rabaul on New Britain. More important, Lae was only 200 miles due north from Allied-held Port Moresby, which was on the Coral Sea.

The air base at Lae became even more crucial to the Japanese as American and Australian troops made slow, grinding progress against enemy ground forces along the north shore of New Guinea's southeastward-pointing panhandle. The base remained a crucial defensive component for the empire as part of the Battle of Buna–Gona. As the calendar flipped over to 1943, the Army Air Forces were being called upon extensively to address General MacArthur's impatience with the completion of that frustrating battle. That included employing an array of medium bombers—primarily B-25s and B-26s—to pound targets from Buna to Lae and in the dense jungles that seemed to be nudging those towns into the sea.

Such a bombing effort as the Port Moresby planes were attempting required fighter escorts. Most of those were supplied by Dick Bong's 39th Fighter Squadron and their fleet of P-38s.

Some of the Lightnings even carried bombs, technically making them bombers, too. That meant they also required escorts. A thousand-pound bomb hanging beneath a P-38 rendered it incapable of being an effective fighter plane.

As the last strains of "Auld Lang Syne" faded away and the new year dawned, the skies above the mountainous jungles would soon be swarming with Allied and Japanese warplanes. Missions came daily. There was little time for rest or downtime.

For his part, Dick Bong had seen little direct action despite abundant seat time. He had gotten a possible third downed plane for his record, but it could not be confirmed. On New Year's Eve, he had been flying bomber escort on one of those many missions over Lae when his squad and he encountered about a dozen Zeros.

Bong quickly found himself with an enemy plane directly in front of him. He had the guy dead to rights. It should have been an easy shot, but the Imperial Japanese Navy Air Service pilot made a sudden skillful move and ducked the shells being hurled his way. Bong did observe a chunk of metal fly away from the Zero's engine cowling as the enemy plane entered a shallow dive. Then it vanished into the clouds. There was no smoke or fire visible. No way to confirm the craft had crashed into the jungle or broken apart in midair.

This one would be listed in the tally as a "probable," but that would not count in any way toward the young pilot's record. The rest of the squadron did shoot down nine of the enemy planes that day, again with no American losses. Bong would mention in his engagement report that the enemy pilots he saw in action that day appeared to be well trained and skillful in how they flew their aircraft. And they were dogged, unlikely to easily give up the fight. They were, as all the instructors had preached and fellow pilots promised, very worthy adversaries. Dick Bong had no intention of underestimating them or their equipment.

On January 7, Bong's squadron was again off on a challenging mission, but this time to attack a different kind of target. Instead of striking enemy troops or airfields, the Lightnings—once more with some equipped as bombers, including Tommy Lynch's plane, and others assigned to be escorts—were after a convoy of ships plying the Solomon Sea, bound from New Britain to New Guinea's north shore. Coast watchers had reported with great confidence the approach of a big flotilla on the way to replenish supplies for the troops at or near Lae and to bring them reinforcements. If the resupply ships made it to the base, it would be a major help to the enemy in maintaining their control and avoiding being pushed back by the Allied troops.

Kenney and Whitehead had decided their bombers and Lightnings would make a concerted effort to see that the convoy never made it into Huon Gulf or anywhere near Lae.

Though the Lightnings were not especially effective as bombers—they were simply too fast to be accurate—Lynch would hit an enemy ship with a bomb that day and sink it. The Lightnings had been most effective in "skip bombing." This was a tactic, partly developed by General Kenney, in which a bomb was dropped as the airplane flew along at near-wave-top height. Then, like a thrown stone skipping on the surface of a lake, the bomb bounced along and, if properly aimed, struck the side of a target ship. There, either it exploded on impact or it dropped into the water beneath the vessel. Then its delay fuse closed and, theoretically, blew out the bottom of the ship. As more pilots were getting trained in the method, and with faster planes like the P-38s and P-51 Mustangs carrying the bombs, skip bombing was beginning to take a toll on the enemy.

Another advantage of using the P-38s as bombers was that once their explosives were dropped, the planes were again fine fighter craft. The airmen could climb back up and join their fellow Lightning pilots to conduct escort duty for the rest of the mission. And that turned out to be an especially good thing in the January 7 encounter.

Looking for the long, frothy wakes of the ships in the enemy convoy could easily have reminded Dick Bong of the times he trailed the scuffs and belly scrapes of a big white-tailed buck in deep snow. But this time, it was a distant swarm of hornets that first revealed the presence of his quarry. As expected, such a crucial procession of ships was not steaming without air protection. Just after noon, with Bong flying top cover high above the medium bombers and bomb-laden P-38s, he saw a dark roiling cloud of about two dozen enemy fighter planes appear out of nowhere. Then the cloud turned as one and zoomed straight for the airplanes that he and his wing mates were assigned to protect.

Dick did not hesitate. He put his Lightning into a steep dive and headed down to do his job while the element of surprise was still on his side.

Almost immediately, though, a Nakajima Oscar spotted him and pulled up to meet him. Meet him literally head-on. Each pilot opened fire on the other the instant he was within range. Bong had heard the scuttlebutt that the Japanese were more than happy to die for their empire and emperor, so long as they took an American down with them. Now it appeared the Oscar pilot was willing to ram Bong and his plane nose to nose if he was not able to shoot the P-38 down first.

Bong stubbornly held his position, still firing away, until he absolutely had to divert one way or the other. Up, down, right, left? His life now depended on the correct move. Bong figured the odds were on his side. Four choices, three of which would be correct. But if he continued straight ahead or if he chose to evade in the same direction the enemy pilot did, it would all be over for both warriors.

Dick nudged the stick to pass just a few feet beneath the onrushing Oscar. But as he did, he saw the enemy plane explode. Bong's salvo had finally found a sweet spot. As bits of the target rattled against his cockpit and nacelle, Bong hurtled on from beneath the enemy craft and turned into a tight circle. He wanted to see if the Nakajima required any more urging to go ahead and crash. He could see what was left of the plane spiraling, twirling, spinning, still breaking apart.

By the time he confirmed his third kill, Bong's fighter-pilot brothers—including those in P-38s who had by then jettisoned their bombs onto targets and hastened up to help with the Japanese escorts—had chased away the rest of the enemy planes. Far below, the sea was littered with the remnants of the enemy convoy smoking or sinking. Or both.

That was not the end of that day's work for Bong and the other members of his squad. If they survived the attack on the convoy and still had ammunition left, they had been ordered to take a very slight detour and strafe ships already in the harbor at

Lae before turning south toward home. They were also to rendezvous with a squad of eight bomb-laden P-38s and help cover them as they dropped their ordnance on various targets at that critical enemy installation.

Nobody expected this job to be easy, either. With the importance of Lae to the Japanese plans for eventually capturing all of New Guinea, they would certainly scramble some fighters to meet any threat they detected heading their way. It took the enemy a while, but they did get more than a dozen planes, mostly Oscars, in the air. They boldly raced closer to the approaching Americans, challenging their attackers with guns blazing and engines screaming.

Almost identically to Bong's engagement with the ill-fated Oscar only a couple of hours earlier that day, another Nakajima came directly at him, as if dead set on knocking the American out of the sky by ramming him if the Japanese pilot did not get him first with his guns.

Bong reacted even more quickly and aggressively this time, diving to meet his attacker before the enemy pilot could get lined up. This time, though, he held his fire until he was much closer, only about half a football field away. A mere fifty yards or so. He was so confident in his ability to aim his airplane, shoot a fatal shot, and swerve to avoid collision that he held off until the last possible second.

The tactic worked. As confirmed by another pilot who observed the action, the Oscar was afire, trailing thick smoke all the way until it crashed spectacularly into the green waters of the harbor below. Kill confirmed.

Bong, however, did not see it. After the shot, he went quickly into a tight loop and then pulled out of a near-wave-top dive to get away from the largest pieces of whatever debris he had unleashed that might now be falling all around him. There was no chance for him to see the damage he had done.

Two skirmishes, two kills, both in one day. As Dick Bong flew back through the rough air that wafted up from the Stanley Mountains, he might well have reflected on his success so far. Had he just been lucky? Some of his fellow pilots had not been as fortunate as he on this day and would never go back home. All it took for a very different outcome was one well-placed enemy bullet. An instinctive but wrong move when ducking while an enemy plane was careening straight for him. A mechanical failure in the aircraft. A moment's loss of concentration while executing a well-practiced but tight maneuver. A misstep in midair that resulted in a collision with another plane, friend or foe. Any one of those occurrences could have changed his day, his life, brutally and permanently.

But the young pilot remained confident. His two additional kills that afternoon had not been mere coincidence. He had skillfully flown a fine airplane and taken two enemy chess pieces off the board. That would not end the war, of course, but every mangled Japanese plane he put into the jungle or the drink made an incremental difference. And that was all he could do to try to shorten that war.

Bong and his squad hurried home ahead of the coming darkness, not just to gloat or brag about the day's accomplishments, though they certainly would do plenty of that. Truth was, they needed to get their planes on the ground, have them inspected and serviced, and get some food and rest for themselves. They did not yet know specifics, but they were aware there was a full mission scheduled for the following day, too. Not much time at all to wind down.

The war for which they had taken so long training had now suddenly become very hot.

And very real.

CHAPTER TEN

THREE KILLS IN TWO DAYS

Thanks to the media, the military, and the movies, the general public has a long-held fascination with the notion of the daring ace fighter pilot. An ace should be dashing, heroic, and artfully skilled in destroying competing aircraft while taking the lead in a brilliantly choreographed but deadly dance amid the clouds.

As generally accepted, a military aviator who is officially credited with shooting down or otherwise causing to crash five or more enemy airplanes while engaged in aerial combat earns such status. The concept originated during the first major war in which airpower played a significant role. That was in what eventually came to be called World War I. That was also the first major conflict in which dogfighting was a commonplace occurrence. Previously, in lesser conflicts, pilots in primitive aircraft fired at one another with pistols.

The French were the first to generally acknowledge and make popular such hero pilots and to decide that five enemy planes would be the qualifying number. This score keeping initially was to help build morale among fighters and the public. Aviator Adolphe Pégoud was the first to be called *l'as*—an ace—by the newspapers after he shot down his fifth German plane.

As would be the case in World War II as well, German pilots had the opportunity to score and confirm far more "kills" than would those flying for the Allies or other nations. This was because most of the air battles occurred over Germany or German-held territory. That made it easier for them to confirm the action when an Allied plane was destroyed. They could simply locate the crash sites later and verify the claimed shoot-downs. The Germans seem to have been very honest about it, too. The Allies had to witness and document the planes' crashes—difficult to do in enemy territory—usually employing a fellow pilot's report or, in later wars, relying as well on film cameras installed in the warplanes.

Another factor was that Germans flew many, many more missions than Allied pilots did. There was no rest for them. And from a strictly mathematical perspective, the Germans had the advantage in numbers of kills by fighting against the Russians. In general, Russian pilots were not well trained and the planes they used were inferior. By far the most numbers accumulated by Luftwaffe pilots were against Russian aircraft.

Also, in World War II, Allied pilots who survived being shot down over enemy-held ground in Europe, and who were able to eventually make their way back to their units, were no longer allowed to fly missions anywhere on the Continent. That was for fear of their getting shot down once again, being captured, and then being tortured into revealing details about those who had helped them escape the previous time. That was typically the French underground or clandestine anti-Nazi groups in other countries. This policy took hundreds of pilots out of contention for ace status. One notable exception was American ace Chuck Yeager, who would go on to become, in 1947, the first pilot to break the sound barrier. After getting shot down over France in March of 1944 and being rescued by the French resistance and extracted through Spain, he was ordered to return home, where he would have been assigned other duties. He had to go all the way to the top to General Dwight Eisenhower, Supreme Allied Commander, to ultimately be granted the rare permission to return to flying his P-51 Mustang fighter over German-occupied Europe. Only then did Yeager earn his ace designation, ending the war with 13.5 Luftwaffe planes shot down.

On the other hand, German pilots could parachute from their damaged and doomed aircraft, land in German territory, and live to fly again, thus having more opportunities to add to their total score. Many did. Some World War II Luftwaffe fighter pilots survived more than a dozen crashes and came back to fight and, in the process, run up their scores. By the end of World War II, several German Luftwaffe pilots claimed more than 300 Allied planes shot down. As noted, the top ace for the US in Europe would be Gabby Gabreski, with twenty-eight kills. (Gabreski would go on to fight in the Korean conflict, during which he was credited with shooting down 6.5 MiGs, making him one of only seven American pilots to make ace status in two different wars.) The top Allied ace of World War II would be Russian pilot Ivan Kozhedub, who was credited with sixty-six kills.

Dick Bong was hardly into keeping track of other pilots' kills. The bid to become the leader in enemy planes destroyed, however, would soon create a considerable number of open and contentious rivalries among many of the USAAF pilots who fought the enemy daily over New Guinea and the Philippines. The spirited competition caught the attention of members of the media, who fanned the flames and enthusiastically began to keep a running score. On the morning of January 8, 1943, Bong ate a hurried breakfast as his squad and he were being briefed. Then, as he took off and rendezvoused with the others above Port Moresby, he was quite aware that one more plane shot down, properly witnessed and confirmed, would officially qualify him as an ace fighter pilot. And America would have one more bona fide hero. He did not need his squad mates, his commanders, or the pesky newspaper reporters to remind him. Nor did he feel the need to brag or promise. He was confident this would be his day.

In truth, he was already a hero. He did not know it yet, but mostly at the behest of General MacArthur, who felt General Kenney was not being generous enough with medals awarded to his men, Bong would soon be awarded the Silver Star. That is the third-highest military award for valor, and the young Wisconsin native was to receive the recognition for his bravery in battle back on December 27. Nor could he have known, as he and his wing mates again raced northward over the mist-shrouded jungle below, that he would earn not only that ace designation but also another high honor, the Distinguished Flying Cross, for what he was about to do on this bright summer day in the Southern Hemisphere.

Bong had reason to be confident. Odds were in his favor this day. Assuming, that is, that he did not get his own plane shot out from beneath him first. His squad and he were bound for the skies over Lae once again. The Japanese ships his buddies and he had helped bomb the previous day had mostly been damaged or sunk, but remnants of the convoy continued on, determined to reinforce and resupply beleaguered enemy units at Lae. Over the span of the next several hours, three different bomber groups were to try to prevent any of those vessels from making it to the port or delivering any cargo or fresh troops. Bong and the other P-38s were to fly high-altitude top cover for all three bunches of bombers.

The first two groups made it to Huon Gulf and dropped their ordnance on the approaching ships as well as on those already at anchor at Lae. They inflicted their damage, all without much more than minor challenges from enemy fighter aircraft. Antiaircraft fire was vicious, but the bombers were at high enough altitude to avoid any serious risk—so long as the enemy did not scramble their own squads of fighters, that is.

By the time Bong and his squad were in formation high above the day's final group of B-17 Flying Fortress bombers, the Japanese had finally managed to get into the air a force of about twenty fighters to intercept them. Once the Lightnings spotted the newcomers, they immediately dived to divert them. They wanted to do this at about 18,000 feet, before the Zeros and Oscars could reach the B-17s' altitude and have a reasonable chance to shoot down some of them. With the sudden attack on the enemy fighters by the AAF planes from high above and out of the blinding sun, the brawl was on.

As he was choosing which of the assemblage of targets he

would initially go after, Bong noticed that one of his brothers was already in serious trouble. A Zero had quickly lined up directly behind another one of the P-38s. The Japanese plane was in a position known by pilots as "on his six," a reference to the six-o'clock angle, or directly behind. Though the P-38 canopy—unlike those on some other earlier fighter aircraft—allowed an undistorted 360-degree view, the six o'clock remained a virtual blind spot. But the other Lightning pilot was now aware, with bullets flying past him and with Dick Bong yelling the warning on the radio, that an enemy plane with deadly intentions was solidly "on his six."

He knew he was in trouble if he could not get away from the Zero and find a better angle. The young pilot had already begun darting, diving, and dodging, doing all he could to try to shake his tenacious attacker.

Bong knew he was likely the best and only hope for the other American pilot. He sent his P-38 directly at a point in the sky where the pair would be in mere seconds, practically locked together in midflight. Then he let loose a salvo, trying to at least cause the Japanese pilot to break off the chase to avoid the barrage.

No luck. The Zero was only a few yards behind the American plane, matching it move for move, firing almost continually.

Bong yanked relentlessly on the stick, worked the foot pedals hard, and somehow made his plane come around to an angle from which he could close on the Zero's "six." Now it was a trio of airplanes, seemingly chained to one another like a roller coaster, flying through smoke and clouds at better than 300 miles per hour.

This time, when Bong fingered the trigger, his bullets hit home. The Zero bucked, jerked, and swerved downward. Jagged shards of metal flew from its fuselage and engine cowling. Then, as Bong pulled up to avoid a collision, the enemy plane erupted in smoke and flame and began to disintegrate in midair. Gravity claimed dominion over what was left.

There was no indication that the canopy might have been sliding open. No parachute. The remains of the Zero hurtled downward, then pelted the dingy waters of Huon Gulf like a passing hailstorm.

Bong's brother pilot, once again breathing, wiggled his wings to show he and his airplane were okay. Then both fliers headed off to find someone else to shoot down.

There were few Japanese planes left, though. In only a few minutes, the Lightnings had eliminated seven of the twenty enemy fighters. The rest had simply flown away, choosing not to engage these odd-looking scavengers that had pounced on them out of the waning sun. Meanwhile, the Flying Fortresses completed their bombing run unscathed and turned back toward their base. Bong and his squad climbed back above the B-17s to dutifully shadow them until they were safely home.

After landing at Fourteen-Mile Field and going through the standard debriefing and report composing, Dick Bong began humbly accepting myriad congratulations for having become an ace fighter pilot that day. He just kept reminding everyone that what he was most proud of in the day's action was being able to get into position to knock that Zero off his buddy's tail.

But he would soon learn that he had earned a couple more

things with that furious action on January 8. Kenney and Whitehead would submit more paperwork on the kid's behalf. That would result in Bong receiving the Distinguished Flying Cross. That decoration is awarded to members of the US Armed Forces who "distinguish themselves by single acts of heroism or extraordinary achievement while participating in aerial flight."

The other reward for a job well done—and for becoming an ace—would be two weeks of leave in Australia. Fellow pilot Tommy Lynch received the same bonus. Kenney later wrote that although he hesitated to take a couple of his best players out of the ball game, he wanted them to "get some rest, get some decent food, and forget about the war for a while."

Unlike the Germans and Japanese, Kenney felt his pilots did their best work when they had opportunities to recuperate from such high-tension duty. Many of his pilots, including Richard Bong, did not necessarily agree. Unless it included enough leave time to go back home, that is.

Whether he forgot about the war or not, Richard Bong did enjoy his time off in Brisbane. Despite his Scandinavian complexion, he took advantage of the warm sun and tropical seas, and according to his letters home, he spent five or six hours a day on the beach. He did not even mind the inevitable sunburn. He knew what the January weather was like back in northern Wisconsin and he intended to make the most of the sunny tropics. Unlike other soldiers on leave, he did not get drunk or hang out in bars that catered to servicemen who found themselves temporarily away from battle. Instead, he preferred swimming— though he did not necessarily like the bathwater-warm salty

water as opposed to the cold, clear lakes and rivers back home—
and relaxing in the warm breeze beneath the palm trees.

He also told his family in his letters that after only a few
days he felt rested and well fed enough that he was anxious to
get back to his unit in New Guinea. He believed he was somehow missing the best part of the action. Bong was convinced
that he could now do an even better job up there. He was inti-
mately familiar with the P-38 and what it could do. His additional practice while serving as a gunnery instructor at Luke
Field had made him an even better shot, almost as if he had the
ability to will the bullets to go where he wanted them to.

Besides, from all he was hearing from fellow pilots who were
also enjoying time off there near Brisbane, General Kenney and
his staff were convinced that a turning point had been reached
in the air war in the region. On January 22, while Dick Bong
was still on leave, the Allies declared that the brutal Battle of
Buna–Gona was over, and it was victory for the Allies.

While the crucial Battle of Guadalcanal in the Solomon Islands would not officially end in an Allied victory until February 9, it was clear that the Japanese had finally given up a crucial
strategic position in the South Pacific, the first chink in the empire's armor to be exploited by the US. And Bong was about to
return to the fray, just in time to play a part in the Allied victory in the Battle of the Bismarck Sea.

The Japanese were certainly aware that the Allies were taking a toll in the skies, too, though bad news often did not make
it all the way to the enemy's top echelon. Under General Kenney, American air assets had become much more organized and
effective in how they operated, even though it was still not easy

taking on an enemy who had the advantages of numbers, dug-in occupation, and near supernatural determination. Their lives did not matter so long as they were sacrificed for the cause of the emperor and the Japanese Empire.

Kenney's reliance on the P-38 Lightnings seemed to be paying off, too, even though there were still issues receiving replacement aircraft and spare parts to keep them in the air.

And pilots. Army Air Forces commanders knew they needed more well-trained and eager young men to fly the limited supply of airplanes they could get. Even in early 1943, Europe was still getting most of the graduating flyboys as well as mechanics and other support personnel.

Still, as Kenney reported to General MacArthur, the Japanese appeared to have gone into something of a lull, at least in the skies over New Guinea. Lae remained an enemy stronghold. However, the interdiction efforts against shipping into and out of the port were slowly choking off that base as well. It was likely the Japanese no longer had enough fuel to keep as many fighters and bombers aloft. And the Allies could only imagine— considering their own resupply issues—how bereft of spare parts and replacement aircraft and pilots the Japanese likely were. But despite the positive trend, the war in the region was far from over. The march across the islands to the Philippines and beyond had only just begun. Even the most optimistic realized it would continue to be a costly campaign. And there was plenty of evidence that the Japanese—even those who had now been defeated on Guadalcanal and in most of New Guinea—were nowhere close to giving up.

As for Dick Bong, even as he medicated his sunburn and

observed the few pounds all the good food, cold Coca-Cola, and lazy beach days had added to his slender frame, he was now well beyond ready to return to duty.

By the last few days of January 1943, he would be back in New Guinea and could begin adding to his score of enemy aircraft destroyed.

CHAPTER ELEVEN

THE COMPETITION HEATS UP

As eager as he was to rejoin the war and begin working toward "double ace" status—ten confirmed enemy planes downed—by the time he was finally back in the cockpit of his plane, Dick Bong could see firsthand the lull in the air war. Plus, two weeks after he returned from leave in Australia, his squad was moved from near Port Moresby to newly secured bases on the north side of New Guinea. Bong would now be flying from the airfield at the former Japanese base at Dobodura, a spot above which he and his buddies had previously done some intense dogfighting. Now that Buna and other areas there were under Allied control, it made sense to base the P-38 squadron at that location. That got them much closer to potential enemy targets at the big enemy installation at Lae as well as those approaching or departing that town through the Gulf of Huon, in the Solomon Sea, and in the Bismarck Sea around the island of New Britain. It also meant they no longer had to contend with the rough air often encountered when flying over the Stanley Mountains.

The move north came about two weeks too late for Bong to take part in the only major action in the area during the month of February. On the sixth, a major Japanese force, apparently aware that the airfields in that area were being built up by the Allies, launched an air attack on Dobodura. About forty enemy fighters and bombers were involved in the daytime assault. American pilots scrambled to meet them and shot down more than half of them. The remaining attackers then flew away. There were no American losses.

Most of Bong's missions, just before and after his relocation to Dobodura, involved escorting cargo planes or conducting reconnaissance runs. Frustratingly, there simply were no Japanese aircraft to shoot down. He wrote home that he would just have to do whatever he was called upon to do for the war effort, even if doing so meant he flew typically boring missions in skies devoid of enemy planes. Bong had no choice. He would have to bide his time until the other shoe dropped, as he knew it inevitably would.

There was plenty of evidence that business was finally about to pick up. With the declaration of victory at Guadalcanal on February 9, the Allies saw indications that Japan had now decided to defend New Guinea even more vigorously. And maybe even go back on the offensive. The empire had to prevent any attempt by the Allies to retake the entire island and use it as a launchpad for their next objective. That meant the empire would have to place even more value on Lae if they were to throw up a very big stop sign. Then they would again try to take all of New Guinea starting from there. At the same time, Rabaul would now be an even more strategically precious foothold for the Japanese. With Guadalcanal lost, Rabaul and Lae were now the primary parapets still standing to block any attempted Allied pushback.

That other shoe finally dropped for Dick Bong on March 3, 1943, when the Battle of the Bismarck Sea began.

Back in December, with things going badly for the Japanese on Guadalcanal and in Buna on New Guinea, and with the Allies' increasing dominance in the air war across the southwestern Pacific region, those in command at Imperial General Headquarters back in Japan had made a fateful decision. They decided to transfer almost 7,000 of their best troops from Rabaul to Lae to reinforce the base there as a first step to capture all of New Guinea. It would require a bold plan, using a convoy of ships steaming directly from Rabaul and across the Bismarck Sea to Lae. The only other option would have required sending those soldiers ashore farther west along the northern coast. That would have been the safer alternative. However, once those troops had reached the beach, they would have found no roads and precious little flat ground. They would have had to march through almost impenetrable jungle and swampland to reach Lae.

Relying on secrecy and speed, a convoy of eight troop transport ships, eight destroyers, and about a hundred fighter aircraft left Simpson Harbor at Rabaul on February 28, making as quick a run as possible, delivering the troops before the Allies even knew what was afoot. Should they have been spotted while en route, whatever opposing aircraft the Americans and

Australians might have been able to hastily scramble could certainly have been rebuffed by antiaircraft fire from the destroyers and by heavy air cover from the skies above them.

Unbeknownst to the Japanese, their plans were not at all confidential. The Imperial Japanese Navy's top secret communications code had been broken even before the war started. The intelligence being decrypted from those messages had proven invaluable at Midway and other sea battles since. Now the US knew exactly when the ambitious convoy left Rabaul, where it was bound, how it was defended, and what it carried. That gave the Allies time to assemble a bomber force with aircraft from the Fifth Air Force. Again, one of those was a P-38 bomber escort flown by Dick Bong.

An American B-17 first located the convoy on March 1. It was steaming furiously through the waters between the west end of New Britain and the village of Finschhafen at the tip of Cape Cretin on the far-northeastern point of New Guinea. The Japanese ships and their valuable cargo were just over a hundred miles from their destination and quickly moving that way.

The first US aircraft launched their attack the next day, while the convoy was still in the Bismarck Sea. Three of the troopships went down. The rest steamed on as darkness ended that day's action.

The next day, the remainder of the convoy, still plowing toward Lae, unwittingly moved to within range of Allied aircraft that had recently been relocated to the northern shore of New Guinea. From Dobodura, Dick Bong and his squad escorted B-17 Flying Fortresses as they launched a thunderous attack. A mighty strike not just against the target convoy but simultaneously on the landing fields around Lae. That was to prevent the Japanese from sending more airplanes to try to defend remnants of the doomed convoy.

By midmorning, the brawl had become even more vicious. As the B-17s approached in waves, dropping bomb after bomb on the ships, Bong and his buddies engaged the convoy's escort Zeros in a sky-filling melee. At one point, he watched in horror as B-17 crew members bailed out of their stricken bomber only to have Japanese fighters zoom in and machine-gun the survivors as they dangled beneath their parachutes. The unfortunate bomber crew members were dead before they reached the sea below. Bong and his fellow pilots were furious, and that led them to fight even harder.

Still, their primary job was to keep the enemy fighters away from the Flying Fortresses. There was no time or place for emotion. Especially now, as Dick and his wing mate came under attack from a half dozen Oscars rocketing in from the thick clouds and smoke.

Bong concentrated on one fighter sprinting his way. He quickly brought his P-38 into as good a shooting position as he could manage. Then he let loose on the Oscar with his nose-mounted .50-caliber machine guns. Bingo! Smoke and fire confirmed the guy was in serious trouble. Bong followed him down, getting off another quick but well-placed volley. He—and his onboard film camera—saw the enemy craft crash straight down into the green waters below.

Bong was already pulling back up to rejoin the fight. Sure enough, another plane—another Nakajima Oscar—blasted past, right in front of him. He gave pursuit, finger already working the trigger. He was close enough to see he had hit the enemy plane's wing fuel tank. The tank that had no self-sealing feature, unlike the tanks on Lightnings. Gas was spilling everywhere. Even if the guy did not go down right away, he would never have enough fuel left to make it to Lae. And at that time, that was the only "friendly" spot within his reach.

As it turned out, Bong would get credit for one enemy plane shot down that day, raising his total to six. The second plane would be listed as "probable." That meant it would not count toward his total.

By the morning of March 4, the Battle of the Bismarck Sea was essentially over. It would be considered an impressive and important Allied victory—one chalked up entirely to airpower. Elements of the US Fifth Air Force and the Royal Australian Air Force had destroyed all eight enemy troopships and sent four of the eight destroyers to the bottom. Some troops were rescued by the surviving destroyers, other enemy vessels that rushed to the area, and Japanese I-boats (submarines). Though Japanese war records would prove notoriously unreliable, they would later indicate that about a thousand troops still managed to make it to Lae while another 2,700 were pulled from the sea and returned to Rabaul. That meant about half the original 7,000 troops on the transports died.

Records differ on how many aircraft were lost by both sides over those three days. Best estimates have ten Japanese fighters confirmed shot down and another nine classified as "probable" kills. Three American fighter pilots died in the four USAAF planes shot down. One of them was Lieutenant Hoyt Eason, an ace who had six kills at that point. Two US bombers went down

Major Richard Bong with his Medal of Honor; photo taken in the Pentagon office of General Henry H. "Hap" Arnold, then US Army Air Forces commanding general.

Bong visits on the steps of the Pentagon with World War I top Allied ace fighter pilot, Eddie Rickenbacker.

The "most shot-at girl in the Southwest Pacific": Marge Vattendahl's college graduation picture on Richard Bong's P-38 fighter in New Guinea.

Richard Bong with Major Thomas McGuire, a fellow P-38 ace pilot who had thirty-eight kills—only two short of Bong's record forty—when he lost his life during the Philippines Campaign.

"Bing and Bong" at the Hollywood Bowl in Los Angeles, a war bond rally featuring entertainer Bing Crosby and Major Richard Bong.

General Douglas MacArthur presents the Medal of Honor to Richard Bong, December 12, 1944.

Bong and his P-38 with decals for enemy planes shot down.

As part of Bong's morale mission, he speaks to trainees and others at Rankin Field, Tulare, California, where he received some of his own early flight training.

Richard Bong visits with a Rosie the Riveter at Globe Shipbuilding Company in Superior, Wisconsin.

Dick and Marge Bong make a honeymoon stop at Lockheed Aircraft in Burbank, California.

ALL THE NEWS ALL THE TIME
Largest Home Delivered Circulation
Largest Advertising Volume

EQUAL RIGHTS
LIBERTY UNDER THE LAW   TRUE INDUSTRIAL FREEDOM

Los Angeles Times

IN TWO PARTS
PART I — GENERAL NEWS

Times Office: 202 West First Street
Los Angeles 53, Cal.
Times Telephone Number MAdison 2345

VOL. LXIV   CC ★   TUESDAY MORNING, AUGUST 7, 1945   DAILY, FIVE CENTS

ATOMIC BOMB HITS JAPAN

Jet Plane Explosion Kills Maj. Bong

Ace's 'Shooting Star' Blows Up in Test Flight Over North Hollywood

Illustrated on Page 3, Part 1

Maj. Richard I. Bong, the 24-year-old Army pilot who shot down 40 Jap planes to become America's foremost ace, yesterday died in the aerial explosion of a P-80 jet-propelled Shooting Star which he was flying on a test flight for the Army's Air Technical Service Command.

A witness said the super-fast airplane of tomorrow blew into flames and exploded 50 feet above the ground in the vicinity of

Continued on Page 3, Part 1

North Hollywood, four minutes after he took off from the Lockheed terminal at 2:30 p.m.

The witness, Mrs. George H. Zana Jr. of 8118 Satsuma St., said she saw a man jump from the plane with his hands over his head. She said she did not see a parachute. An instant later, according to her story, the crash literally disintegrated in a flaming explosion which caught the pilot in the air.

Other Witnesses

With three men, also witnesses to the crash, Mrs. Zana raced to a vacant lot where the flying parts of the ship landed. They saw Bong's body about 100 feet away from the plane's fuselage, wrapped in flames.

It was obvious that "the curly-headed winner of the Congressional Medal of Honor and the "hottest" combat pilot in the nation's history, was dead.

Although Mrs. Zana saw no evidence of a parachute as the figure leaped from the plane, charred remnants of a chute were still attached in bits. Bong's body, it could not be determined, according to Army officers at the scene, whether he had attempted to "hit the silk" from such a low altitude or whether the parachute pack had spilled open when his hurtling body hit the ground.

From Frank Bokenhamer, Lockheed service mechanic who watched Bong hit the jet plane into the air, came this description of the tragedy:

"We always watch those Shooting Stars take off, Maj. Bong took off normally, but as he passed the control tower we noticed a man on the observation platform of the tower run around on the other side to watch the plane.

Terrible Sight

"We knew something was wrong when we saw a puff of black smoke come out just as he leveled off in flight. The right wing seemed to tip a little. The black smoke may have been the escape hatch came off. The plane started into a glide and then sort of nosed over straight down. We saw a column of smoke go up in the air about 400 feet. It was a terrible sight."

As soon as Bong was airborne, it was learned, he contacted the control tower at the

Turn to Page 2, Column 4

FEATURES INDEX

Yanks Give Germans New Privileges

Rights to form local unions and engage in political activities—almost forgotten rights for Germans—were granted by Gen. Eisenhower in American occupied zone of Germany. Turn to Page 5, Part 1.

AMUSEMENTS. Page 1, Part II.
COMICS. Page 11, Part I.
FINANCIAL. Page 8, Part I.
HOFFER. Page 4, Part II.
POLLYANOKE. Page 4, Part I.
RADIO. Page 8, Part II.
RATION POINTERS Page 3, Part II.
SOUTHLAND. Page 3, Part II.
SPORTS. Page 8, Part II.
WEATHER. Page 6, Part II.
WOMEN. Page 5, Part II.

Death Ends Career of Sen. Johnson

Californian Fought to Last Against All Foreign Alliances

WASHINGTON, Aug. 6.—(AP)—Sen. Hiram Warren Johnson died today, fighting to the end the battle against tie-ups with foreign nations which he began a quarter-century ago in the bitter battle against the League of Nations.

Death, attributed by his physician to thrombosis of a cerebral artery, came at 6:40 a.m. in Bethesda Naval Hospital.

The 78-year-old California Republican, a national political figure since early in the century, had been under treatment there for two and a half weeks. He was in a coma when the end came.

Opposed Chairer

One of the Senate's last official acts was in cast its one vote in the Senate Foreign Relations Committee against ratification of the United Nations charter for a world organization of nations.

Even after the count of his fatal illness his vote was recorded against final ratification through a pair with two charter supporters, Sens. Reed (R.) Kan., and Thomas (D.) Ida.

(Pairs of senators require two Senators declared against one, because of the two-thirds vote required for ratification.)

Committee Factor to End

The silver-haired Johnson, long a free-founding debater in the Senate, had been heard seldom on the floor in recent months. But he was still a factor to be reckoned with in committee affairs.

His death cut wait a handful of votes against 8000 votes. Elected to the Senate in 1916 after six years as Governor of California, Johnson was ranking Republican on the Foreign Relations

Turn to Page 2, Column 6

INVENTORS CLAIM GADGET WILL PEEL, FREEZE AND WASH

CHICAGO, Aug. 6. (AP)—An electric appliance manufacturer said today a combination clothes washer, potato peeler, dish washer and ice cream freezer will be on the market early in 1946.

Edward N. Hurley, president of the Hurley Machine Household Utilities, said the gadget will sell for less than standard power washing machines, can be operated daily as a dishwasher and potato peeler, and can be converted to a clothes washer by an attachment, which the housewife can convert in less than a minute.

Another unit with an oil-or-compartment for ice and electric refrigeration by dry-ice as long as you want it frozen. The LaVallette was part of a bombardment group providing

B-29's Pound Navy Arsenal on Honshu

New Raid Follows Wiping Out of Jap 'Mystery Town'

GUAM, Aug. 7. (UP)—A force of 125 B-29's attacked the Toyokawa naval arsenal on Honshu Island with high explosive bombs at noon today, Gen. Carl A. Spaatz announced. The raid followed two days of heavy aerial bombardment which all but wiped out a Japanese "mystery town" Sunday in what may have been an attack on a newly developed Japanese rocket-launching installations.

With long-range fighters from Iwo Jima as escorts, the Superfortresses hit Toyokawa and Japan's few remaining arsenals for the first time. It is on the South-Central Honshu coast, 80 miles southeast of Nagoya.

Enemy Raid Disclosed

The Strategic Air Forces chief gave no details of the last strike, which came shortly after the dispatches disclosed that the assault by more than 400 armed yards direct from the north during last night's fighters and bombers of Gen.

LONDON, Aug. 6. (AP)—The London Daily Mail said tonight in a Washington dispatch quoting "reliable sources" that Japan would be served with a new ultimatum to surrender within 48 hours or face obliteration from the atomic bomb.

The Daily Mail said the ultimatum will say: "We will withhold use of the atomic bomb for 48 hours, in which time you can surrender. Otherwise you face the prospect of the entire obliteration of the Japanese nation."

"Workers had to use tongs 50 feet long in extracting the mercury column. It is taken at extremely high temperature. An unusually large amount of the metals involved in the control area—

Turn to Page 3, Column 5

Four Bandits Beat and Rob Actor

Louis Adlon, film player and brother-in-law of Marion Davies, and his mother, Mrs. Hedwig Adlon, of former film star, were robbed of $180 cash and $2000 in jewelry early yesterday by four bandits who forced his car to the curb on the Sunset Strip and then beat and robbed them.

Adlon, husband of Rose Davies, but just left a party at a nearby apartment house and was driving to his home at 325 Ocean Front, Santa Monica, when the attack occurred.

Destroyer Blast Claims 21 Lives

WASHINGTON, Aug. 6. (UP)—Twenty-one men lost their lives when the destroyer LaVallette struck a mine Feb. 14 in Manila Bay, the Navy announced today. Further the Osaka radio announced the demolition of a cruiser in the Philippines. Fourteen more were wounded. The LaVallette was part of a bombardment group providing

Man's Most Destructive Force, One Equal to 2000 B-29 Loads, Blasts Nips

WASHINGTON, Aug. 6. (AP)—The most terrible destructive force ever harnessed by man—atomic energy released by the disintegration of uranium—is now being turned on the islands of Japan by United States bombers. The Japanese face a threat of utter desolation and their capitulation may be greatly speeded up.

Existence of the great new weapon was announced personally by President Truman in a statement issued through the White House today. He said the first atomic bomb, invented and perfected in the United States, had been dropped on the Japanese army base of Hiroshima 16 hours before. Hiroshima is on the main Japanese island of Honshu, 450 miles west of Tokyo.

That one bomb alone carried an explosion more violent than 2000 B-29 Superfortresses normally could carry to an enemy city using not these T N T bombs.

Atom-Splitting Test by Science Group Disclosed

Secretary of War Stimson followed through with a report that the blast offered a cloud of smoke and dust over Hiroshima so impenetrable as to make immediate, accurate observation of results impossible. The power of the bomb, Stimson said, is such as to "stagger the imagination." He asserted it would, "prove a tremendous aid" in shortening the Japanese war.

Old Speculation on Air Attacks Revived

Stimson's emphasis on this point renewed speculation all over again as to whether Japan may be completely crushed by air attack without invasion.

Mr. Truman noted that the Japanese rejected the surrender ultimatum from Potsdam, and that this had been intended to spare the Japanese people from "utter destruction."

Now, he said, with the new bomb, the Japanese "may expect a rain of ruin from the air the like of which has never been seen on this earth."

The announcement heralded an Anglo-American victory at a cost of $2,000,000,000 in one of the grimmest battles of our war—the battle of the laboratories—to unlock the secrets of the atom and yoke its energies to military use.

The Germans were striving desperately to win this highly secret contest in the closing months of the European struggle.

New Epoch Seen for War and Peace

Scientists agreed that a new epoch in both war and peace probably is at hand. Although much experimenting remains to be done, this newly controlled energy doubtless can be used also to drive rockets, planes, ships and trains for constructive as well as destructive purposes.

President Truman said the new bomb, which draws its energy from the same sources as the sun, has more power than 20,000 tons of T N T, itself a tremendously powerful explosive. Since one 25-20 ordinarily can deliver about 10 tons of bombs to a target, that means 2000 Superfortresses would be required to accomplish with T N T the destruction that one plane with one of these new bombs can achieve.

By another standard, Mr. Truman declared the bomb has 2000 times the blast power of the 11-ton British "Grand Slam" bomb—the most concentrated bundle of destruction previously known on the earth.

In fact, in evaluating the enormous power involved in this new weapon, the President had to reach beyond the limits of the earth for comparison.

"It is a harnessing of the basic power of the universe," he said. "The force from which the sun draws its power has been loosed against those who brought war to the Far East."

Warning Prepared by Churchill Issued

This line appeared to hold dramatic possibilities for propaganda against the Japanese. They regard their Emperor Hirohito as a direct descendant of the sun goddess. Perhaps they can be told that the very power of the sun itself is being turned to their destruction.

Following the announcement in Washington Prime Minister Attlee issued in London a similar statement which had been prepared by former Prime Minister Churchill before he left office.

"It is now for Japan to realize in the glare of the first atomic bomb which has smitten her," Churchill said, "what the consequences will be of an indefinite continuation of this terrible means of maintaining a rule of law in the world."

The text of the highly secret weapon was carried out in the morning of July 16 in the New Mexico desert about 120 miles southwest of Albuquerque. The flash was so brilliant that a blind girl in Albuquerque was reported to have cried aloud "What was that?" The War Department said ten men who were standing six miles away were knocked down. President Truman, as he was nearing American shores aboard the cruiser Augusta, homeward bound from the Potsdam conference, and Secretary Stimson worked together on the

Turn to Page 2, Column 1

JAP BROADCAST NOTES TRUMAN ANNOUNCEMENT

SAN FRANCISCO, Aug. 6. (AP)—A Tokyo Japanese Domei Agency broadcast noted in a broadcast picked up here by The Associated Press that President Truman had announced the dropping of the atomic bomb on Hiroshima.

The Japanese Ambassador to the United States and Japan's chief enemy to the new type of bomb used in the broadcast, recorded by Domei's own Communications system which monitored Washington radio.

The Domei broadcast said the enemy was using a new type of bomb in its raids on Japan. The broadcast was aimed at a few days before the latest bomb.

A Lockheed P-38 fighter aircraft similar to the one piloted by Dick Bong.

as well. A total of thirteen Allied lives were lost, including those shot as they parachuted from their damaged bomber.

There would be no more attempts by the Japanese during the war to reinforce Lae, or, for that matter, any other location in New Guinea. They decided to take a new stand elsewhere in the Southwest Pacific.

It was another obvious turning point. And the crew members of the Army Air Corps units were justifiably proud of what they had accomplished.

Once they were incentivized with bounties such as cases of fine Scotch for reaching certain milestones, it was inevitable that the pilots would engage in spirited competition for accumulating the most kills. Some of that rivalry was not necessarily lighthearted. Some of it was downright foolhardy. Even though he tried to get as many enemy planes as he could, Richard Bong would not be a willing participant in any hot race to run up a score.

Buzz Wagner had been the top gun in the Pacific with eight kills before he went back to the States and died in that mysterious plane crash in the Florida Panhandle. Tommy Lynch would have fifteen when in mid-1943 the USAAF sent him home for some rest and to train other fliers. He would subsequently add five more to his count upon his return to the war later that year.

Some of the newcomers to the fray would be even more focused on tallying a high score. One of those was Lieutenant Neel Kearby, a Texan and, at thirty-one years old, easily the "old man" in the group. Unlike most of the other "kids" flying for Uncle Sam, he had a wife and children back home. He headed up a squad of P-47 Thunderbolt fighters. That happened to be a type of plane that approached the capabilities of the P-38, was more readily available at the time, and had strong advocates among leaders in the Army Air Forces. However, the Thunderbolt had one significant shortcoming. It was more limited in its operating range than the P-38s. The Lightning crews poked fun at the Thunderbolts, saying thunder was merely an obnoxious sound that followed lightning.

To settle the differences of opinion surrounding the two very different fighter planes, a mock dogfight was authorized. Kearby would fly the Thunderbolt. Dick Bong would pilot the Lightning. The half-hour demonstration proved little, other than that the P-47 was very near the P-38 in air-to-air combat capability. Advocates for the Thunderbolt felt Kearby had narrowly defeated Bong. Those backing the Lightning maintained their guy and plane had won, but not by much. Bong's official account of the battle tells us nothing other than that the showdown did occur.

Kearby would make the most of the P-47's considerable capabilities, though. He would be credited with twenty-two enemy planes destroyed and become the first USAAF pilot to be awarded the Medal of Honor.

Another challenger was Tommy McGuire, who had undergone training at about the same time as Dick Bong. He had spent time in Texas while Bong was in Arizona and California. Though they had not yet met, they would soon be embroiled in a heated race for the top spot on the kill list. Heated from McGuire's perspective, that is.

McGuire reached New Guinea in April of 1943, taking the same route and likely the same transport airplane as Bong, but he would not fly his first combat mission until August. Before his time was up, McGuire accumulated thirty-eight kills. That meant he would eventually finish second to Bong as the top American ace of World War II.

Each of these young men was a remarkably brave and talented fighter pilot, determined to do his best to help win the war against a fanatical enemy. Each was unselfish and did what had to be done. Each found himself yanked from the war periodically to recharge his batteries, and they all complained about it to anyone who would listen. How could a real fighter jockey become the top ace in the war if he was getting drunk or painfully sunburned on the beach in Brisbane? Or if he had been shipped back home to market war bonds or teach rookies how to avoid augering in while in the cockpit of his trainer? Each of those eager young men pushed himself and his warplane a bit too forcefully at times, whether trying to shoot down the opposing pilot before getting shot down himself or to add another tally to his list of kills.

While most of the pilots competed stridently with one another, Dick Bong often deliberately did things that kept him from adding to his score.

In a notable example, General George Churchill Kenney was visited in his office by one of his young pilots. The kid had a strange complaint. A grievance that Kenney, in all his days of military command, had never heard before.

"General, you've got to do something about Bong," the pilot grumbled. "He's giving away Nips!"

CHAPTER TWELVE

REWARDING THE WINGMAN

D ick Bong rarely admitted being scared up there. However, in a letter home in mid-March—and though he could give no details because of censorship limitations—he admitted he had experienced fear during a particular recent skirmish. One that occurred in the steamy tropical skies almost directly above his new home base at Dobodura.

That recently established airfield, being one of the closest to the big enemy air base at Lae, seemed to be especially irritating to the Japanese. That meant attacks trying to neutralize the US base came often. Typically, those strikes were small and mostly ineffective, almost halfhearted. USAAF fighters were usually able to get into the air and chase the enemy away with only minimal damage done but a number of Japanese attack planes taken out.

The attack on March 11, 1943 was not typical. Two dozen Japanese medium bombers—Mitsubishi G4M Type 1 attack bombers, nicknamed "Bettys"—with more than twenty Zero and Oscar escorts suddenly appeared amid the rain clouds over "Dobo." USAAF aircraft, including Dick Bong's, were not able to get into the air before bombs were already falling. The swarm of enemy warplanes was ignoring antiaircraft fire and aggressively strafing the airfield. Bong and his partners were not able to get high enough, better than 20,000 feet, and give chase until the bombers had already dropped their complement of destructive ordnance and were turning back northwestward, toward Lae.

He and his squad decided, despite the weather, to go after their fleeing attackers. Typically, the Bettys were at their most vulnerable as they tried to get themselves lined back up in close formation while picking up their escort fighters and then powering back toward home. However, on this mission, they would not be that far at all from their destination. That meant there would certainly be more enemy fighters coming to meet them and hit back at the pursuers once they realized the returning Japanese bombers were fleeing an angry and sizable flock of American P-38s.

The enemy escorts were still there when the Dobo squadron got to altitude. Bong would later write in his report that he had immediately fixed his attention on the last G4M in the formation and had aimed his own guns at the unfortunate bomber. However, before he could open fire, he was surprised to see that at least a half dozen Zeros (some might have been Oscars but there was not much opportunity to be precise in identifying them) had taken special interest in Bong's Lightning.

No time to shoot at a fleeing bomber! Time to duck and parry!

He pointed his nose almost straight down in a frantic dive. He would later report he reached an airspeed of almost 475 miles per hour, about fifty miles per hour faster than the P-38 was designed to fly without putting dangerous stress on the bird. With great effort, and far closer to the jungle treetops than he really wanted to be, he bottomed out in his dive. Then, without hesitation, he pointed skyward to face the flock of pursuers, even if he was outnumbered six to one.

There, directly above him, was either the same covey of enemy planes or a new bunch determined to knock him down. This time, he put his plane into an amazingly tight banking circle, practically standing on his wingtip as he flew up and away from the jungle, across the beach, and dangerously close to the wave tops. It galled Bong to appear to be running away from a fight. That was not what he was doing at all. He would soon show them what his intentions really were.

Bong was completing a turn that would bring him right back into position to cut loose on the Zeros. Once he was in the position he was looking for, he pointed his P-38 directly at the closest target and, convinced he was close enough to be accurate, he fired.

Direct hit!

Smoke and debris filled the sky. The enemy fighter was crumbling as Bong pulled back hard on the stick to try to avoid the cast-off wreckage. He even employed body English to try to will his fighter to avoid what was left of the enemy plane.

No time to do any fancy avoidance gyrations, though. There were at least five other opponents coming his way. He picked out one of them, the one he could target most easily, and fired off a blast.

Another hit. And then, with a waggle of his wings, Bong

turned just enough to aim directly at a third enemy fighter. He activated the trigger with an especially hard squeeze, as if that would make the bullets fly faster and with more deadly force. It must have worked. The targeted Zero's engine began belching fire and smoke and hot metal. Surely it was a goner, too.

Now, as Bong pulled out of his dive, it appeared to him that the other fighters were either chasing somebody else or had climbed back up to where their bombers were still attempting to make their escape. That was, after all, any escort's top priority: shielding the bigger planes all the way back to Huon Gulf and the base at Lae. He could see that the first two planes he had shot were clearly crashing, out of control, afire. The third, the last one he had hit, still had smoke trailing from its engine but appeared to somehow remain under power, maintaining altitude with its propeller whirling as it flew off in the direction of its home base and a safe landing.

No real chance to tail that one to confirm if the guy made it or not. Bong would never know. More important to turn back to assist his buddies. Oh, and to confront the three Zeros that were now coming to meet him. And that were already peppering his fuselage with bullets.

He had been hit. Not for the first time. But obviously with more damage inflicted that time.

Bong made an abrupt bank to his left, disappearing into a convenient cloud, hoping to be able to assess the situation and decide whether to bail out or nurse his plane back home. His left engine was damaged. That much he could tell immediately. The instruments showed it was running hot, losing power. His natural instincts confirmed what the gauges were telling him.

He feathered the left engine, relying on the right-side one to maintain adequate airspeed to overcome drag and gravity. Enough forward impetus to keep him aloft. Enough to get away from those dogged Japanese pilots who seemed fixated on him, as if they knew who he was and what a threat he was to them. Enough to get him the short distance back to Dobo without having to give up on his ride and parachute out of the cockpit and into shark-infested waters. Or into some of the densest and most unforgiving tropical forest on Earth with headhunting inhabitants.

Any other fighter plane in use by the US at that time, its single engine knocked out, would have been a lost cause. However, Bong's Lightning—bullet pocked and smoking but still with one perfectly functioning Allison engine—made it home that day for repairs. He would fly again in a day or two. He had collected two of the ten confirmed enemy kills that day. That raised his official score to eight.

The hastily scrambled group from Dobo also shot down one of those fleeing bombers. The Americans lost one P-40 and its pilot as well as one P-38. Its pilot, who had equaled Bong's two kills that day, was able to bail out and be rescued.

Dobo had taken some serious punches. Parts of the runway were scarred by bombs, making for tricky landings for the returning elements of the 8th and 9th Fighter Squadrons. Several men on the ground had been killed or wounded. Even though everyone sensed there had been a turn in the war, this surprisingly strong raid showed once again that the Japanese had not yet ceded New Guinea to the Allies. This one-hour set-to was more confirmation of a tenacious enemy, one who would fight to the death before surrendering. This would not be the last of such assaults out of Lae. Every one of them made life dangerous for the new Allied air bases that now surrounded the only Nippon stronghold remaining on the island.

The remainder of March 1943 was relatively uneventful for Bong. Except, that is, for the presentation to him of his Silver Star for his action just after Christmas. The citation read, in part, that it was for his performance while serving as a "Fighter Pilot with the 9th Fighter Squadron, 49th Fighter Group, FIFTH Air Force, (then 370th Service Squadron, attached to 39th Fighter Squadron, 35th Fighter Group), in action against the enemy near Buna, New Guinea on 27 December 1942. Lieutenant Bong was a member of a flight of four P-38 airplanes which engaged a flight of fifteen to eighteen enemy aircraft at Dobodura, near Buna, New Guinea and destroyed seven of the enemy planes. Lieutenant Bong personally destroyed two of the enemy airplanes. His gallant actions and dedicated devotion to duty, without regard for his own life, were in keeping with the highest traditions of military service and reflect great credit upon himself, his unit, and the United States Army Air Forces."

Dick did make several long escort patrols in March but encountered few potential targets. On March 28, having just completed one of those long runs the day before, he was off duty, getting a day's rest. That just happened to be the day of another major pushback against enemy planes, ones attacking a new Allied base at nearby Oro Bay. Bong's fellow Flying Knights did just fine without him, claiming thirteen enemy aircraft with only the loss of a single P-40. And Dick made sure he was right there on the edge of the runway to welcome his buddies back and congratulate them on their success that day.

Then he was back in the cockpit the next morning, patrolling near Oro Bay, just in case the enemy decided to try again. There was no sign of them until Bong's wingman spotted a lone aircraft in the distance. At first, they could not be sure if it was friend or foe. Then, as they flew closer, they could easily see the big red emblem and identify the loner as a twin-engine Mitsubishi Ki-46, a "Dinah." That aircraft was typically used by the enemy as a reconnaissance aircraft.

Bong assumed the plane was trying to assess and confirm the damage that might have been done at the base at Oro Bay during the action the previous day. Many of his fellow fighter pilots might not have considered a Dinah a target worthy of the expended ordnance necessary to bring it down.

Not Dick Bong. It was an enemy airplane. It was contributing to the Japanese war effort in some way. It needed to be removed from service. Violently.

With a quick hand signal to his wingman, Bong sent his P-38 into a steep dive to intercept the target. The Japanese pilot, flying without escort and in a plane that was fifty miles per hour slower than a Lightning, put his Dinah into its own dive, trying to find as much speed as he could to attempt to get away.

It was fruitless. On his first pass, Bong already had one of the Dinah's engines afire. After his second run, the Ki-46 was falling apart in midair. And Bong had his ninth kill, one tick away from being designated a double ace.

By this time, nobody needed proof that Dick Bong was an exceptional fighter pilot. General Kenney had been back in Washington during this most recent action, but when he returned and heard what had been going on, he promptly promoted Bong to the rank of first lieutenant. But there would soon be an incident that showed Kenney that one of his top fighter pilots might be even better at his job than his score showed.

At about this time, another young flier from the squadron who had been Bong's wingman on a mission sought an urgent appointment with the general in his office. As Kenney would later write, the pilot had a most unusual accusation.

"Bong is giving away Nips," he charged.

Kenney did not understand and requested clarification.

"In that fight today, I followed Dick down on a bunch of Zeros. He fired a burst into one of them, and as he jumped for another, he called to me to finish off that first Nip. Without thinking, I fired, but as I did, I saw that the Jap's wing was already coming off and the whole plane was on fire. When we got back this afternoon and we were writing up our reports, Dick told me he saw the plane crash onto a coral reef and that he would certify it for me. I tried to tell him it was his Nip. He was already gone by the time I made my first shot. His wing was falling off and on fire before I hit him. 'Oh, no,' he told me. 'He's yours. I just grazed him. He probably would have gotten away if you hadn't finished him off.' General, tell me what I ought to do. He wrote in his report that it was me that got it. He told me if I don't get credit nobody will. He's really being stubborn about the whole thing. And this is not the only time he's given away

Nips either. Every wingman he's ever had will tell you the same thing."

Kenney could only smile. He told the young pilot that any such decisions were between him and Bong, that the ace likely recognized the value of good wingmen, appreciated the many things they did to help him shoot down enemy aircraft. That was Bong's way of making sure they got credit for all they did, even when they were not technically the ones who fired the shots most responsible for the kills.

Kenney would also later declare that Dick Bong gave away at least one kill for every two he officially claimed. And understanding the farm boy's reasons for being so generous, the general heartily approved of such a creative and morale-enhancing calculus.

CHAPTER THIRTEEN

TEN AND ELEVEN

Dick Bong became a double ace a few days later. The Japanese had decided to concentrate aerial attacks on Allied shipping bringing supplies, ammunition, and reinforcements to the region as MacArthur's "stepping-stone" move to the west was getting underway. It was April 14, 1943, when the enemy sent a considerable force of aircraft down from Rabaul, aimed at ships around Milne Bay on the far eastward point of New Guinea and just north of the Coral Sea.

Best estimates were that the attack included three dozen regular bombers, two dozen dive-bombers, and at least thirty fighters. About the only thing good about such a large force headed their way from such a distance was that it was easily detected well before it arrived. Everyone from shore watchers to Allied ships and radar saw the oncoming menace. A response consisting of more than forty fighters was sent from various Allied bases to deflect the Japanese. That included eight P-38s, all that the AAF bases could get into the air at the time due to the lack of spare parts.

Dick Bong was in the cockpit of one of those Lightnings. He was among the first of the defenders to claim a victim. That happened to be one of the enemy bombers.

Bong's wingman that day would later testify that two more of the big planes should have rightfully been credited to the new double ace. One of them, with its engine set afire by bullets from Bong's guns, appeared to be in real trouble. Another suffered multiple hits and was badly crippled. However, it was a cloudy day, and everybody was busy. No one witnessed those two enemy planes go down.

The force was diverted all right. The AAF planes knocked many of the foes out of the sky. The American pilots claimed that three fighters and ten bombers were taken down. Bong got official credit for only one of the bombers with his nifty diving move, boring in from out of the bright tropical sun just above the cloud deck before the shielding enemy fighters even saw him coming.

That constituted his tenth confirmed shoot-down. He was now officially a double ace.

General George Kenney would later express his considerable relief that Bong, the limited number of serviceable Lightnings, and the other planes in the defense force had been able to drive the enemy back to the north. And he was thankful that the Japanese remained unaware of the dire straits in which the Army Air Forces found themselves at this point in the action around New Guinea.

It was also clear that the Japanese were no longer trying to claim more territory. Or aiming to control the Coral Sea or shipping lanes to and from Australia. Their mission now was to hold on to the islands they already controlled and to maintain the line should the Allies try to advance from New Guinea and the Solomons and reclaim territory on the way to liberate the Philippines. Had the Japanese known the depleted condition of the USAAF air fleet, they would surely have been more aggressive. The empire's navy remained strong, but many planes and trained pilots had been lost. American victories at Guadalcanal and the Bismarck Sea (the Japanese public, and many in the military, did not hear any word of the latter defeat until after the war had ended), combined with their inability to take all of New Guinea, amounted to a wake-up call and a change in emphasis for the Japanese. The big challenge was to try to protect their shipping in the region. Dug-in occupation troops, naval ports, air bases, and more—all at the far reaches of captured and controlled territory, distant from the Home Islands—depended on those vessels for supplies, ammunition, and reinforcements if they had any hope of hanging on to hard-won ground.

Only after the war did the Allies learn that Admiral Isoroku Yamamoto, commander in chief of the Japanese Fleet, was never aware that his forces had been so handily rebuffed by Bong and his mates on April 14. To the contrary, the reports he received crowed that the effort had resulted in a glorious victory, inflicting heavy damage on many American vessels in Milne Bay, including several military ships. That had become typical after such defeats. The exaggerated claims, totally inaccurate estimates of ships and planes destroyed and casualties inflicted, were only to please Yamamoto, the rest of the upper ranks of the

Japanese military, and, of course, Emperor Hirohito, who was often insulated from the true state of the war.

It was only four days after Bong tallied number ten that Admiral Yamamoto, at great risk to his personal safety, decided to see for himself how things were going in the South Pacific. Reports he was hearing did not seem to match up very well with reality. From Rabaul, he climbed aboard a Mitsubishi G4M Betty bound for several stops, including an air base near Bougainville, the largest island in the Solomon Islands archipelago, for a first-hand inspection. US Naval Intelligence caught wind that the mastermind of the attack on Pearl Harbor, the architect of the Japanese Navy's air superiority, and its top commander was making the run. They had the admiral's full and precise itinerary.

A squad of P-38s—the only fighters with enough range to pull off such an ambush—left Guadalcanal to go looking for the highly desirable target. Even President Roosevelt had reportedly gotten word of Yamamoto's trip and personally approved whatever mission it took to get revenge for December 7, 1941. That included those Lightnings flying only thirty feet above the waves for most of the way to avoid radar detection.

It was a successful run. Yamamoto's Betty was intercepted, attacked, and shot down by one of the P-38s. The admiral's plane crashed into the jungles of Bougainville. His body was found by a Japanese rescue party the next day and positively identified.

The Japanese, of course, had not given up. Determined to keep the Allies at bay, they began building up airpower at Wewak, another port on the north side of New Guinea. By the end of 1943, it would become the largest enemy air base on the island. That expansion included launching regular bombing and strafing runs on Dobodura and other AAF and Australian bases along the coast and all the way down to Port Moresby. They dispatched a relatively big force for an attack on Dobo on May 12 and again the morning of the thirteenth. But once more, P-38s rebuffed the enemy, took down almost half their planes, and suffered only minor damage to the base. Two American planes were lost but both pilots survived.

To his great disappointment, Richard Bong missed that frantic action, too. He was out of town, once more on one of George Kenney's forced vacations.

It would be June 12 before any other significant contingent of enemy aircraft tried to approach the base. That was almost two months after the major failure of the assault out of Rabaul and the loss of the empire's top naval commander. It was also a full month after the attacks out of Wewak on Dobodura. Even then, it was slim pickings for Kenney's boys. A lone reconnaissance plane—maybe attempting to get some idea of the actual condition of American airpower there—approached, escorted by a couple of Zeros. They flew overhead in the dark of a moonless night. Such runs were typical, but the Japanese planes usually flew in fast and at low altitude to avoid detection, took a look, then hastily turned and headed back home to Wewak at top speed. Other than waking up sleeping personnel, no damage was done. This time, though, radar caught the intruders early enough that P-38s had the opportunity to scramble in response and confront them. All three enemy planes were shot down, crashing into the sea off the Huon Peninsula near Lae as they attempted to make it back home.

Dick Bong got one of the fighters. That was number eleven.

Bong was delighted to be there and in the air for this bit of action. He had been on the beach in Australia on furlough since May 3. That meant he had missed the substantial assault against Dobo on May 12 and 13. His commander had sent him away from the war for three reasons: because he felt the intense kid needed some rest to maintain a keen edge (though Bong denied any fatigue), because he wanted to reward Bong for reaching double-ace status, and because the AAF, at the time, had no serviceable P-38 for him to fly. Dick had returned to Dobo from leave only on May 16 and flew a mission the very next day. A mission in which he did not see a single enemy airplane, a phenomenon that had become frustratingly common.

But by that time, more P-38s were approved for the Pacific. With the significant help of "Rosie the Riveters," the planes were finally being produced in significant numbers. The AAF's efforts in protecting Allied shipping had certainly helped, too. Replacement parts were becoming more reliably available all the time. So were well-trained rookie pilots.

Because of the availability of planes, pilots, and spare parts, there was some much-needed reorganization of the structure of the Army Air Forces in the Pacific in mid-May. That included the creation of a new group that would fly P-38s exclusively, the Fifth Air Force's 475th Fighter Group. Those units had already proven their value, even when they did not have the quantity of planes or pilots to adequately do the job. And Kenney remained convinced that having them available and in the air was crucial to the plan to island-hop toward the Philippines, the Marianas, and Taiwan, as General MacArthur was demanding.

There would be many more air and sea battles to fight. Though carrier-based planes had already proven their inestimable value, land-based warplanes like the P-38s would be essential in attacking, capturing, and maintaining control of the enemy-occupied islands that lay in the projected path of the Allies' push. More than ever, the war effort would also depend on twentysomething-year-old pilots to take the war to the Japanese. Boys like Richard Bong.

And the fair-haired Wisconsin farm boy was about to pull off a most unusual feat—one that would only enhance the legendary reputation he was building.

CHAPTER FOURTEEN

STRAFING A CROC

O nce a myth is created, it often evolves, growing greater and greater on its own. That is especially true in such environments as war in which the media and the public are eager for inspiring or colorful stories. Often whether they are proven true or not.

The mythlike narrative of Richard Bong, the quiet farmer's son from the American heartland who blew enemy warplanes out of the sky by flying as close to them as possible before shooting, was already ripe for exploitation by mid-1943. People back in the States as well as in other Allied countries were hungry for good news and positive stories about heroic people. Bong fit the bill, and the papers were more than happy to supply what their readers craved.

Double aces made good copy regardless. And this clear-eyed, clarinet-playing (Dick had brought his high school instrument with him to the South Pacific and often played tunes for his fellow airmen, to mixed reviews), milk-drinking straight arrow who just happened to be taking a significant toll on a despised enemy would soon be associated with yet another intriguing story by reporters hungry for headline fodder. This colorful tale would contribute considerably to Bong's stature as an almost mythical hero.

Never mind that it might never have happened.

On June 2, 1943, Bong and his squadron were heading back from a routine—and benign—patrol out over the Solomon Sea and in the vicinity of the Japanese air base at Lae. Preparations were already underway for a ground, naval, and air assault on the base to put it out of business once and for all. By this point, the enemy had clearly decided to move most of their New Guinea air assets farther west, to remote Wewak. General MacArthur was keen on finally taking the remainder of the big island, and controlling Lae would be a major step in the effort.

That morning, though, while nearing Dobo and the conclusion of the routine mission, one of the P-38 pilots in Bong's squad, Lieutenant Paul Yeager, broke radio silence briefly to report a major mechanical malfunction in one of his engines. They had encountered no enemy fire, neither from plane nor antiaircraft guns, at any point during the run. Something had simply broken in the motor. But Yeager was convinced he would not be able to nurse his bird back to Dobo and get it safely on the ground without risking crashing it and maybe damaging other planes or facilities.

He had no choice. He would have to abandon the aircraft and parachute into the dense jungle below.

They were not that far from base. Bong noted the general area where Yeager settled into a small clearing near a big lake and radioed a request for a spotter Piper Cub to come look for his partner. A ground rescue party was also to be sent out. Bong suggested that the best way to quickly reach the downed pilot might be by boat, across that lake, not by hacking a way through the dense rain forest.

There was some urgency. First, they had no idea whether Yeager had been injured when he hit the ground. But more concerning was the fact that the Japanese often fired on survivors and their rescuers if given the opportunity. And the pilot had gone down not that far from Lae and territory sometimes still patrolled by enemy troops. For that reason, Bong and one of the others in the squad hurried on to Dobo, refueled, and then rushed back to fly cover for the Cub and the rescue efforts.

Several sources later reported that the rubber boat with three rescuers—fellow pilots, as was often the case—was nearing the shore of the lake where a thankful Yeager waited. But then a new and unexpected hazard presented itself. And it did not wear a Japanese Army uniform.

From his position overhead, Dick Bong and the circling Cub pilot both noticed what appeared to be a log floating along behind the little rubber boat. Men on the boat saw it, too, and one later reported he thought it was a native canoe adrift. But both men high above knew immediately what it was. And the danger it presented.

It was a crocodile.

Without hesitation, Bong put his P-38 into a dive, descending almost to the water's surface as he approached the boat. Then, when close enough, using the same strategy usually reserved for Zeros or Bettys, he cut loose on the critter with his 20mm cannon (some sources maintain he used one of his 50-caliber guns), blowing the stalking croc to smithereens. An uninjured Yeager was quickly collected; then he and his rescuers made it safely back to base.

There were jokes aplenty about the alleged incident once it was over and all were safe. Speculation about whether a crocodile kill should be included in a pilot's tally of enemies destroyed. About whether Bong should have gone back and tried to collect enough of his victim to construct a nice piece of luggage. More than likely not enough was left even for a belt for the slender young pilot.

Newspapers all over, and especially in Australia, ran with various versions of the story once they got wind of it. The Brisbane *Courier-Mail*, for example, beneath the front-page headline, "Lightning Strikes 'Gator,'" breathlessly reported, "A United States fighter pilot has become a foundation member of the Alligator Club. With cannon fire from his Lightning [he] killed a giant alligator trailing a rubber boat containing three pilots on a rescue mission."

The story went on to reveal that it was Richard Bong who took out the "alligator"—in that region, it almost certainly would have been a crocodile and the reporter simply had his reptiles confused—and the impressive note that the pilot had shot down ten enemy planes to date.

Questions remain about whether the remarkable incident really took place. In addition to the newspaper coverage, Carl Bong Jr. would later relate a very similar incident in a book he compiled about his brother, but with some slightly different details. He indicated that he heard the story from someone who was actually there at the time, giving the narrative a bit more validity. The tale has also been recounted as truth in several historical works about the war in the region and in at least two YouTube videos, but no film footage has ever surfaced.

However, in his official report on the day's mission, Bong makes no mention of any crocodile execution or even having fired his weapons at all that day. Pilots typically gave that information in detail in their logbooks. He briefly and straightforwardly told of completing a two-hour mission and then having flown "cover for [a] search party." That was the only indication by Bong that anything out of the ordinary had happened.

True or not, the purported incident only helped add to the now growing legend of "America's newest ace of aces." And soon, even as Bong's kill count continued to climb, George Kenney would receive a report of one more example—and one that was absolutely truthful—that demonstrated what a remarkable and courageous pilot the kid was. Details of one of the most selfless and stunningly brave midair incidents the general had heard about in his more than a quarter century in aerial warfare.

One that only confirmed his early confidence in that blond-haired, baby-faced Swedish boy with the innocent blue eyes.

CHAPTER FIFTEEN

FOXED AT 10,000 FEET

Most of June and well into July of 1943 brought yet another dry spell for the fighter squadrons of the Fifth Air Force in New Guinea. The USAAF was not sitting back and taking it easy, though. General Kenney had decided he needed operational airfields closer to Lae to support the increased efforts to neutralize the base. But he also wanted to be able to reliably reach and address the growing Japanese air presence at Wewak, even farther to the northwest up the coast. Those distances from his existing bases were a stretch, even for the longer-ranged P-38s.

Unlike with Dobodura, Port Moresby, and other AAF installations, the best choice for the primary new US airfield would be inland, in Morobe Province, and on the northern side of the Stanley Mountains. From there, it would be only a short hop to Lae, close enough that the fighters could confidently drop their external tanks for combat maneuverability, or even make runs there and back without ever installing them. It also would place the airfield only about 300 miles from Wewak, again easily within reach of the P-38s with their auxiliary fuel tanks.

However, since the proposed site was not near the coast and far from any sizable location for marshaling construction equipment, manpower, and supplies, everything necessary for the construction of the base had to be airlifted aboard C-47 Skytrain aircraft, primarily from Port Moresby. And those big, slow birds would require escort fighters. When carrying a load, their cruise speed was only about 160 miles per hour. That duty kept Dick Bong and his fellow P-38 pilots busy during the lull, even if it was disappointing to those craving air-to-air skirmishes and the chance to enhance their kill scores.

The new base was named for the nearest village, Tsili Tsili. However, General Kenney bucked that decision, maintaining that the pronunciation of the place—"silly silly"—was not appropriate for an Army Air Forces location. He insisted on calling it Marilinan, the name for another cluster of native huts nearby. As it turned out, both names showed up interchangeably in official USAAF records.

Kenney also ordered a clever diversion by faking construction at a spot farther to the northwest along the hip of the big mountains. He told members of the 871st Airborne Engineers to send a small contingent to that location and "raise some dust" to convince the Japanese the new base was being constructed there. The ruse worked. It would be mid-August, more than a month after fighters began running regular missions out of Tsili Tsili/

Marilinan, before the Japanese finally discovered the actual aerodrome from which all those brutally heavy air attacks were originating.

It would appear to the casual observer that this was quite a bit of wasted effort simply to have an airfield within easy range of the two primary target locations. Construction equipment such as bulldozers and trucks had to be dismantled, loaded on the C-47s, flown over the Stanley Mountains, landed at nearby marginal airstrips, unloaded, then hauled to and reassembled at the construction site. Every construction worker, heavy-machinery operator, spare part, stick of dynamite, and bite of food had to be flown in through the thick clouds that shrouded the peaks of the Stanleys, one of which topped out at more than 13,000 feet. But the decision eventually proved to be a good one. The base with the silly name but perfect geographical location would ultimately play a key role in the Allies' finally taking control of New Guinea. (After the war, Tsili Tsili was abandoned and eventually reclaimed by the jungle. Any signs of the base or the many men who served there are difficult to find today.)

Most of the P-38 jockeys were bored with the Skytrain escort duty. They rarely encountered any enemy planes, and the flights from Port Moresby to the area of the new base were both tedious and dangerous. Dick Bong was not vocal about the monotonous but essential missions. It was part of the job. Yes, it was preventing him from adding to his shoot-down total, but as he noted in letters to the family back in Poplar, he did not care so much about that sort of thing. He would do whatever it took to win the war. Including babysitting Skytrains.

Things got considerably less dull one morning as he and five other P-38s once again escorted a dozen C-47s heavily loaded with equipment and supplies. They had crossed the highest of the mountains and were over the Benabena Valley, not far from their destination and already descending through 10,000 feet, when one of the Lightning pilots spotted a flock of eight Ki-43 Oscar fighters. They were hastily approaching from the north, flying at about 15,000 feet. Bong was the wingman for Captain Sidney Woods that day. The pair made up what for this mission had been dubbed "Green Flight." The other three Lightnings, in formation a short distance away on the other side of the C-47s, were "Blue Flight."

As the Oscars rapidly drew closer, three of them suddenly peeled away as if they had lost interest in any kind of fight. But the other five buzzed ahead, directly toward Blue Flight. Their intentions were obvious. Bong and the others knew the Japanese pilots were homing in on the bigger group of protectors, hoping to draw them away from the unarmed C-47s, leaving a hole for the other trio to drive through for an attack on the transports before Bong and Woods could respond.

Dick Bong was not about to allow such a thing to happen. He banked hard to aim his P-38 directly at the five oncoming Oscars. It was only seconds before he was close enough to draw a fine bead on one of them. He fired a burst of .50-caliber bullets, and he could see they had hit home.

But before he could determine if he had inflicted any significant damage, he saw from the corner of his eye that three of the Oscars were now on his tail and closing quickly. His reaction was automatic, based on plenty of training and even more real-world experience. He threw his airplane into a sharp evasive turn and powered from that into a steep dive, boring right into a convenient rain cloud.

Flying blind and buffeted about by turbulence, he pulled back on the stick and put his plane into a gravity-defying climb, hoping nobody else was hiding in that same section of cloud. When he broke into the clear at the top of the thunderhead, he spotted another Oscar directly in front of him. He had the chance to get off only a short barrage before yet another Ki-43 came surging directly at him from behind. With a quick move, again by instinct, he ducked downward and right back into that same bumpy cloud.

Once again, when he emerged, he found himself usefully lined up in a good position to fire at an Oscar that seemed to have been placed there just for him to conduct some target practice. Bong gratefully took what he had been given.

This time, he was certain he saw two explosions on the target: one in the area of the engine, the other along a wing. And as he zoomed past, Bong was convinced that one was mortally wounded and going down.

Then he noticed something just as threatening as the Nippon fighters. His gasoline gauge was almost on the "Empty" peg.

Though he hated to leave his buddies to finish the fight without him—he had seen enough to know that they had the upper hand and that the C-47s, with their continued shield, would likely make it to a safe landing—he had no choice. He pointed his Lightning toward Dobo, hoping he would not have to try to land as a glider instead of as a proud fighter under full two-engine power.

He was thankful that both props were still turning when he set down on the runway at Dobodura. Bong grinned but he still felt bad about deserting the brawl back there. And not being able to confirm whether either of the two Oscars he had shot had crashed. Indeed, he would not be credited with shooting down either Oscar he was sure he had hit that morning.

But then, as he pulled off the runway and started to taxi toward the barn, both Allison engines abruptly sputtered and quit. They had slurped up the very last drops of gasoline. He coasted as far as he could, then climbed out to await a couple of guys running his way to help him push the aircraft on home and to the end of the mission.

That was when Bong noticed several large bullet holes clean through both wings. None had hit anything vital, but they had come frighteningly close. Running out of fuel had not been the biggest threat he had faced that day after all.

While some of the other squadrons would finally engage in serious fighting toward the end of July, it would be July 26 before Dick Bong's Flying Knights found themselves in the middle of some of the most frantic action most of them had seen so far. Bong led a group of P-38s on a run to Lae as well as to the enemy airfield and garrison in the tiny town of Salamaua. It was a routine bombing-and-strafing raid, all in preparation for the soon-to-come assault on the two bases by American and Australian ground troops. Those vital enemy installations would ultimately fall in September.

The July 26 mission remained typical, with no sign of enemy aircraft until after the Knights did their damage at Salamaua and then turned inland, over the Markham River Valley. That was where they encountered plenty of company. Easily thirty-five enemy fighters suddenly appeared in the distance.

Bong was the first to notice that some of them were the new Kawasaki Ki-61 fighters, designated "Tonys" by the US War Department. They so closely resembled the German Luftwaffe's Messerschmitt Bf 109 fighters that Allied intelligence had at first believed the Japanese had acquired some of those excellent warplanes from Hitler. The big concern with the Tonys was that Allied pilots would no longer be able to get away from enemy fighters simply by diving. The Ki-61 was perfectly capable of giving chase, regardless of the depth and speed of the evader's dive.

But now, because Bong and his squad were outnumbered and surprised by the sudden appearance of such a large force, there was no time to contemplate the capabilities of their adversaries. Bong dropped his auxiliary fuel tanks for more maneuverability and went to work, deciding which plane he would shoot down first.

He selected a Tony and opened fire. And missed.

A hard dive, a bottom out, and a steep climb left him head-on with another plane, this time a Zero. As always, Bong aimed his P-38 at the enemy, and then, when he was close enough that he felt he could not miss, he shot.

He did not miss this time. The Zero was immediately ablaze and coming apart.

A quick bank left Bong staring right at a Tony, maybe the

same one as before, ahead of and below his own plane. It was in almost perfect position for a shot. At first, he thought he had missed the Ki-61 again. But that was not possible. Bong's tracers had gone right into the new plane's belly.

Then, as he moved even closer, ready to shoot again, he saw big hunks of metal flying away from the plane's fuselage. Flames erupted from somewhere inside the craft. Smoke was everywhere. The Tony was a goner.

Before Bong could savor that victory, another Tony approached from his right, crossing directly in front of him at about the same altitude. This one would be remarkably easy. He fired. It was as if someone had set off a keg of dynamite in the engine of the Kawasaki. The plane was burning and beginning to awkwardly tumble downward, out of control.

The first Tonys Dick Bong had ever seen, and he had just shot down two of them!

But again, no time or opportunity to celebrate. There remained an abundance of enemy planes out there doing their best to send Bong and his Lightning to a similar fate. And a sky full of targets for him to aim at and shoot.

Sure enough, in the distance, he spotted a lone Zero looking for something to attack. Bong goosed his engines, found the same altitude as the unsuspecting Japanese pilot, and maneuvered into position for the perfect aim directly in front of the snout of his P-38. When close enough, he let loose with a five-second burst from the .50-caliber. The bullets hit home. The plane's canopy flew away, giving Bong a good view of the enemy pilot furiously trying to get his aircraft under control. But then the engine cowling flew off the Zero, and the whole front of the plane exploded, spewing fire and smoke as the nose tilted radically downward, toward the unforgiving jungle two miles below.

After following his victim down a few thousand feet to be sure the enemy pilot had no hope of recovering, Bong climbed back to where the action had been so fast and furious. That was no longer the case. He could see only other P-38s, the pilots of each futilely looking for more targets just as eagerly as he was.

Nothing. No enemy planes.

The entire encounter had lasted less than half an hour. In addition to Bong's four kills, other members of the 9th Fighter Squadron had claimed six more. In his official account of the day's action, Bong would sardonically report that there were so many enemy planes in the sky above the Markham River that he and the other USAAF pilots "couldn't help but hit something" if they merely fired their guns.

It was only a minor disappointment to Dick Bong—but something he would not dwell on—that he had not gotten a fifth enemy plane that day. Such a feat carried its own term: being an "ace in a day." Few American fighter pilots would earn such a designation.

After that day's action, Bong had fifteen verified kills. On the scoreboard, that put him in a tie with the USAAF's top fighter pilot, Major Tommy Lynch, who was, at that time, still back in the States enjoying some R & R at the command of General Kenney.

The general continued to proudly reward Bong, who remained one of his favorites. When he heard Dick had claimed a quartet of enemy fighters on one mission—including two of Japan's newest and most effective aircraft, the Tonys—he promptly put in paperwork to award the kid another Distinguished Flying Cross. He also promoted Bong to the rank of captain.

It was only two days after the four-kill day when Bong would distinguish himself yet again and even further impress Kenney and others with his valor, quick thinking, and extraordinary piloting skills. And this incident had nothing to do with numbers on a score sheet.

On July 28, Bong was part of a flight of nine P-38s sent out to escort bombers for an attack on a flotilla of Japanese destroyers and supply barges in the Bismarck Sea north of New Britain. In the process, and as the B-25 bombers very effectively did their job below, the Lightnings encountered a throng of enemy fighters attempting to protect their ships. There were at least fifteen of them, all Oscars as far as Bong and his fellow Knights could tell.

The fight was on. In minutes, Bong had riddled one of the escort Oscars, sending him plummeting downward into the sea. Enemy plane number sixteen for the Swede. And one of eight Japanese fighters taken out that day by the Flying Knights.

In the throes of battle, even as he flew about, dodging pursuers and looking for more possible targets, Dick Bong took notice of another bit of drama taking place right in front of him. One of the other P-38s was clearly in trouble, with an engine already trailing heavy smoke. The pilot was doing all he could to make it to a cluster of clouds. From there, he might be able to avoid more destruction and then limp home on the remaining engine.

One of the Japanese fighter pilots, though, already smelled blood. Bong could see an Oscar had assessed the situation and was now diving on the maimed P-38. Instinctively, Bong could tell the enemy airman had the right angle and speed to intercept the

Lightning before its pilot could duck into the clouds. And with the bad engine, he had no hope of eluding his assailant.

With a quick cut, Bong steered his own Lightning into a steep plunge that would bring him between the fleeing P-38 and the diving Oscar. He knew he could get into a place where the Japanese pilot would either have to fly through him or consider Dick a better target than the other Flying Knight. No doubt he would then let go of the damaged plane—it was surely crashing—and take the easier shot at Bong's plane.

To add to the enticement, Bong pulled a neat bluff. He feathered his left engine. That would convince the Oscar pilot that the newcomer was also in trouble, down to a single engine, making him just another attractive but much closer sitting duck. Bong even waggled his wings, as if he was having difficulty keeping his Lightning in level flight. He did all he could to sell the idea to allow his buddy the opportunity to escape into the clouds and then head for home.

The ruse worked. The Japanese pilot abandoned his chase of the other P-38 and angled in to take down what he believed to be the easier target. The Oscar began shooting and Bong felt some of the bullets jarring the plane as they bit in. But he concentrated on restarting the left engine and simply flew away from his bamboozled adversary, an opponent who must have known at that point that he had been hoodwinked. Because of the speed of a fully functioning P-38, the enemy flier knew there was no point in giving chase in his much slower Ki-43.

As it turned out, the drama was not quite over. After pulling off that bit of successful chicanery, and with the rest of the enemy fighters now gone, Bong set a course back to Dobo, mission accomplished. But his P-38 suddenly began to shudder violently. At first, after a scan of the instrument panel, he had no clue what might be wrong. The jolting got worse and he knew he needed to quickly find a place to set down or he might soon be taking a parachute ride.

The new airfield at Tsili Tsili was not officially completed and open for business yet, though the first P-38 units were already officially based there and had begun cautiously using the runway. It was the closest airfield. And it was a damn sight better for landing a misbehaving airplane than the alternative: tangled jungle and mountainous terrain. Bong steered his convulsing aircraft in that direction and radioed a terse heads-up so nobody there would think he was a lone attacking Japanese plane, and try to shoot him down.

As he flew toward the base, he twisted around in the cockpit, looked back, and was shocked at what he saw. Half his tail section was gone!

The guy he had snookered had extracted at least a modicum of revenge after all. That explained the vibration. But Bong could also see that his ailerons—the hinged flight control surfaces that were part of the trailing edge of each wing—were also badly damaged, some missing, some dangling. If he even made it to the runway, all this destruction was really going to make the landing interesting.

He had no choice. He flew on.

Somehow, Bong managed to make his descent while wrestling his airplane into alignment with the runway at Tsili Tsili. With great physical effort, he brought it down, touching the ground without bouncing too much or landing sideways. Then bringing her to a stop but only after running off the far end of the landing strip and ending up nose down in a drainage ditch.

That was when he realized that one of his three tires was flat. And that he had no brakes.

He shook his head, checked himself, and decided he was not hurt. That were no flames about to devour him. But his Lightning was surely done for, a total loss. That was disappointing. He knew how desperate the Fifth Air Force was for functional P-38s. And he had just broken one beyond repair.

Later, when the wreckage of Bong's plane was dragged off to salvage spare parts—nothing related to the P-38 was ever discarded if it could be reused or repaired—everyone back at the base learned just how lucky one of their top aces was that day. The thick armor at the rear of the cockpit had done its job well. It was dented from multiple bullet strikes, any one of which would have killed the pilot had the thick metal shield not been there. Workers counted more than fifty bullet holes in the wings and fuselage, many of which were within millimeters of important control cables. The two primary fuel tanks in the plane had been punctured by multiple gunshots. Only the unique rubberized self-sealing system had kept them from leaking or bursting into flames, which would have been fatal.

When Bong was asked about how he had managed to cheat death that morning, he changed the subject. He wanted to talk only about how that Japanese Oscar pilot must have felt when he realized he had been so effectively tricked. And how Bong and his Lightning had suddenly zoomed away from the startled enemy flier, even after suffering all that damage.

"I'll bet the guy was wondering what kept that P-38 flying," he told his buddies. "And I bet he really was mad when he figured out that I had foxed him into thinking I had a bad engine."

Bong was also happy to learn the pilot who actually had suffered the bad engine had escaped and nursed his plane safely back home.

Bong also had very little to say about that day officially becoming the top-scoring ace in the entire US Army Air Forces.

CHAPTER SIXTEEN

HUNTING SEASON

While it may not have seemed like it to the Japanese, Richard Bong was not the only American pilot who was putting an end to Japan's air superiority over New Guinea, New Britain, and the far reaches of the Southwest Pacific. Despite being late to the fray, seriously outnumbered, and not nearly as well equipped initially, other elements of the Army Air Forces along with the US Navy were finally beginning to win the air war in the region.

A good example was Lieutenant Colonel Neel Kearby, another of General George Kenney's favorite pilots—"This keen-eyed lad looked and sounded like money in the bank to me," Kenney wrote—even if he did not fly the general's favorite aircraft. Kearby and his group of P-47 Thunderbolt fliers had at last started to make a dent after receiving and assembling their aircraft, getting delivery of the proper auxiliary fuel tanks, and taking to the skies. The initial ground assaults on the enemy air base at Lae by US and Australian troops started with intense bomber runs to soften up the resistance. The Thunderbolts were well suited for those attacks.

Even with good equipment, though, it was still those with the most talent who did the most damage. On one mission, Kearby and his wingman spotted an enemy fighter and a bomber flying close to each other. Kearby proceeded to knock both aircraft out of the sky with one quick burst of machine-gun fire, even before his wingman could get off a shot.

On another afternoon, Kearby set a new USAAF record for the number of adversary aircraft shot down by one plane in a single day's action. Previously, the most kills by a lone plane in one day had been five. But in frantic air-to-air fighting over Wewak, the sharp-shooting Texan dispatched six enemy planes—four Oscars and two Tonys—in quick succession before running low on fuel and being forced to head home. He almost certainly got a seventh victim that day, but other members of his squad were so involved in their own scuffling that they did not witness the end of the fight. There was no other way to confirm the feat since Kearby's camera had run out of film just as the first of the bullets from the P-47 slammed into the enemy plane's engine cowling. No visual verification, no credit.

General Kenney was so disappointed by the episode that he personally visited the unit responsible for the film cameras on the fighters. He wanted to determine for himself how Kearby's camera had not captured and documented the end of his amazing feat. The gun camera crew apologized but told the general that there had never been the need for that much film before. They promised, however, to make certain in the future that Kearby and others who were likely to need it would have enough celluloid to capture at least seven shoot-downs. The cameras simply would not hold any more film.

General Kenney promptly submitted his recommendation for the Medal of Honor for Kearby. The US Navy pilot who had set the previous record of five kills had received the medal, so Kenney felt his man should, too. General Douglas MacArthur would personally present the award to Kearby in January of 1944. As previously noted, that gave Kearby the distinction of being the first Army Air Forces pilot to receive his nation's highest award for valor in action against the enemy.

For the next few months and into 1944, and to no one's surprise, Kearby kept pace with Dick Bong and several more in total number of enemy planes destroyed. As with the other top fliers, it was obvious he possessed the special skills required to take advantage of his aircraft and its weapons to shoot down enemy planes while avoiding their counterfire.

However, in the process of taking down another victim on March 5, 1944, again near Wewak, Kearby would come under attack from an Oscar. Likely mortally wounded and his plane no longer flyable, he crashed into the thick jungle below. Kearby died there from his wounds, leaving behind a wife and three children. His body would be recovered in 1947 by a Royal Australian Air Force search team and eventually returned to North Dallas, Texas, for burial.

Another pilot who had begun collecting plenty of enemy scalps was Tommy McGuire. For a number of reasons, McGuire would not be able to demonstrate the promise his instructors and fellow pilots had seen in him during his training until August of 1943. In addition to health issues, the big holdup for McGuire was the frustratingly limited supply of P-38s, the plane he had been trained to take to war, as well as the dearth of spare parts to keep the birds in the fight. His first real combat action came in a big way, though, as part of a series of massive raids on Wewak and other nearby auxiliary Nippon airfields on August 17 and 18, 1943. In an operation that would become known to the Japanese as the "Black Day," more than 150 of their aircraft were destroyed, most of them while still sitting parked in neat rows on the apron adjacent to the runways. Speculation was that the Japanese had a different problem from the Army Air Forces: plenty of airplanes but not enough pilots trained and ready to fly them.

McGuire got no official credit for damage done while strafing planes on the ground on that first day. But when the enemy managed to launch some of their fighters during the second morning's attacks, he was able to shoot down three of them in his first truc air-to-air action. And he would add two more kills in his second mission, making ace status in only a couple of runs. That was enough to earn him a recommendation for a Distinguished Flying Cross.

Now the young pilot could proudly paint five Japanese flags on the nose of his P-38, right next to the moniker *Pudgy*, which he had given the plane. That was his pet name for his wife, Marilynn, who impatiently waited for him back in San Antonio. By the end of August, McGuire would have seven kills along with recommendations from his commanders for both the Distinguished Flying Cross and a Silver Star.

Fulfilling his earlier promise indeed! The only thing Tommy McGuire ultimately needed to justify all that confidence in his abilities was a ride that carried guns.

The same could have been said for Dick Bong. After riding his badly mauled Lightning off the runway at Tsili Tsili, he found himself without a plane to fly. There were only dim hopes for getting a new one anytime soon. He would be stuck on sixteen planes shot down until another shipment of Lightnings arrived from Burbank. When it was learned that a ship was due to arrive any day down at Brisbane, he caught a ride and went down to wait on it. After all, General Kenney had promised the very first Lightning to arrive would be his. As soon as it was assembled—they were shipped mostly as parts, like one of Bong's boyhood models—he could head north and rejoin the war.

The general would later write of another conversation he had with Bong. To make Dick feel better about the wait for his replacement plane—and since his top pilot did not give a whit about his score and had told his boss that he was not in a race with anybody—Kenney pledged that when Dick got his twentieth shoot-down, he would be awarded with two months' leave.

"I told him he could go home to Wisconsin and shoot at some deer instead of Japs," Kenney recalled. "The kid grinned and told me that if he could just get a plane to fly, he'd hit twenty by the middle of November and that was when deer hunting season opened back there."

As it happened, the cargo ship showed up in Brisbane the next morning and Bong was flying his new ride back to New Guinea in only a few days. Flying at top speed, he arrived just in time to be briefed and join his squadron on a bombing raid on an airfield in now-familiar territory in New Britain. Bong was excited about the likelihood of encountering opposition on such a run over territory so long held by the enemy. Maybe even enough that he could claim all four enemy planes he needed to cash in on the general's bribe.

Bong and his squadron bombed and strafed viciously but the only enemy fighters they saw were on the ground and soon in flames. But as they turned toward home base, Bong spotted a lone plane in the distance. Not a fighter. A relatively swift reconnaissance plane. Probably a Mitsubishi Ki-15 "Babs," a type the Japanese were replacing with more up-to-date models but would one day soon bring back as "kamikaze" attack craft.

The plane was an enemy target. Armed? Maybe. But worth shooting down. Dick Bong put his '38 into a steep dive and attacked while others in the flight watched. Number seventeen, downed and official. And with still a month left before the start of hunting season in the Badger State.

Attacks on Rabaul near the end of October would ultimately give Bong the targets he needed to reach his goal.

The Japanese had captured the area in January of 1942 and, because of its strategic location, immediately began building up a huge presence there, despite the city of Rabaul being within sight of one of the planet's most active volcanoes. The harbor itself had been formed by the flooded caldera of another. (Years later, in 1994, Rabaul would be severely damaged by a violent eruption from the harbor volcano.) Intending to first control shipping to and from Australia, then to eventually take that continent, the Japanese initiated major air, ground, and naval operations from there. Other planned action would seek total control of New Guinea, the Solomons, and more for the Japanese Empire.

However, as Allied airpower steadily gained control of the skies, and Allied ground and naval forces finally halted enemy advances and began retaking territory, the Japanese decided to draw down forces at Rabaul, moving them to Wewak and other areas to the west. Those forces at one point had numbered more than 110,000 troops and thousands more support and command personnel.

That troop withdrawal gave the Allied forces the opportunity to chase the enemy out of New Britain altogether. After the former and formidable enemy base at Lae fell to the Allies in September, regular and intense aerial assaults pounded both Rabaul and Wewak. In mid-October, General Kenney launched one of the largest air assaults of the war so far against Rabaul. It included almost 350 aircraft, among them more than 200 bombers and 125 Lightning fighters along as escorts. Damage was extreme, but enemy fighter response was nil. No opportunity for any of the P-38 contenders to improve their scores.

There would soon be other promising chances, though. Dick Bong was part of another huge attack on Rabaul on October 29. He had been along for another raid five days before, escorting B-25s as they inflicted horrible damage on the beleaguered base. Although records show that P-38 pilots on that run took out more than three dozen of the empire's aircraft, Bong did not score. His report dryly reported that though he had shot at and likely hit three, he could not claim any of them.

But after midday on the twenty-ninth, just as Bong and his squad reached the target area and the bombers began wreaking havoc, the sky suddenly filled with Zeros. Bong picked out a likely target and motioned for his wingman to follow him as he climbed to take on the enemy pilot. But then both he and the wingman were startled to see that three more Zeros had somehow gotten on their tails and were already firing.

Bong utilized his favorite evasion move, a steep dive the Zeros dared not attempt. Sure enough, the chasers stayed at altitude, looking for other targets as Bong pulled up a mere thousand feet above the choppy waters of St. George's Channel, between the islands of New Ireland and New Britain. There, he spotted another Zero likely looking for a target of his own. Somehow, the Japanese pilot had not seen Bong's spanking-new Thunderbolt leveling off directly ahead of him and at close range. Before the Flying Knight's adversary was likely even aware of the P-38, Bong had blown the other plane apart and was climbing, looking for more.

And there they were! Two other Zeros, but not as oblivious as Bong's most recent victim. He took on both. It turned out to be quite the set-to. Both enemy pilots were well trained and damnably determined. Hoping that none of their friends would join the party, Bong dived, ducked, banked, and shot. Shot many times. But every time he thought he had one of the Zeros dead to rights, the guy made a sudden darting move that left him unscathed.

Finally, with a hard turn and a stiff climb, Bong got one of his quarries right where he wanted him and sent him tumbling downward into the channel. As Bong made a tight move to try to find the other plane again, he had a disconcerting realization. With all the shooting he had been doing with this pair, he was out of ammunition. He had nothing to throw at the Zero but a cannon shell from the 20mm, and he would never hit the Zero with that.

With the enemy plane a few hundred feet away, making a turn to try to reengage, Bong goosed his engines and easily pulled away. The Zero had no hope of catching him as Bong regretfully set a course for Dobo.

Two more enemies sent into the sea would have pleased most fighter pilots. Bong's extending his total to nineteen—one short of what he needed to earn a trip home for Christmas—should have made him consider the mission exemplary. But Bong was disappointed he had not taken down that last Zero after expending so much ammo trying.

He would have plenty more chances during furious action that would come over the next six days of major attacks against Rabaul. However, as with everything else in this war so far, it would not be easy. The Japanese had spent the better part of two years reinforcing their positions there on the edge of the Bismarck Sea. That included digging and carving out deep tunnels and reinforced bunkers into the volcanic rock above the harbor. They fully intended to hold this base until the very last marine was dead and every fortification reduced to rubble. Also, to prevent such a defeat and the humiliating loss of a key base, the Imperial Japanese Air Service continued to fly in large numbers of reinforcement aircraft, even as the USAAF reduced plane after plane to burning hulks.

In late October and early November, Bong and his mates were surprised by the stiff resistance they met. Nine P-38s and six USAAF bombers were lost in a run on November 2. Dick Bong was a part of that mission but unable to claim a victim. His P-38 teammates, though, blasted more than forty enemy fighters out of the sky while gunners aboard the B-25s took down two dozen more in their own self-defense.

On November 5, the Army and the Navy threw what they hoped would be a knockout punch. They launched their first coordinated attack involving both carrier-based aircraft and the usual land-based USAAF planes, mostly from New Guinea. Richard Bong commanded one of the P-38 flights headed that way.

The Navy planes struck first, shooting down twenty-five Japanese fighters. Then what remained of the enemy Zeros and Oscars quickly landed, refueled, and took off again. Their pilots' usual tactic was to trail the naval aircraft back to their carriers and then attack those big flattops.

By the time Bong and five dozen P-38s and twenty-seven B-24 Liberator heavy bombers showed up, there was little resistance besides ground-based antiaircraft fire. Only about a baker's dozen of enemy fighters scrambled to meet them. Dick Bong pounced on the first Zero at which he could point his snout and took him out with one quick burst from his .50-caliber gun. As soon as he was certain that the bird was a goner, he got behind another Zero and promptly sent it to the same fate.

Two short shots, two kills. No wasted ammo this day.

One dark cloud over that mission, though, was that Dick's wingman, George Haniotis, was shot down during their tussle with the Zeros. Though he was spotted afloat on his life raft in the sea by one of the other pilots, by the time Allied PBY rescue aircraft reached the area, Haniotis was nowhere to be seen.

Maybe because of that loss, or more likely because he was rarely effusive over such things in his official reports, there is no indication in Bong's incident report or logbook for that day that he was especially elated at having gotten numbers twenty and twenty-one. Just the usual technical descriptions of deflection angles and ammunition expended, and terse details of damage done. No mention that he had now exceeded General Kenney's requirement for earning some downtime. Or that he was already within five enemy planes of equaling consensus hero Eddie Rickenbacker's "unbreakable" record.

By the time the general received word of Bong's accomplishments, the kid was off on yet another run to Rabaul. Again, Bong and his squad encountered unexpectedly robust resistance from enemy fighters. Despite the number of targets, Bong did not shoot down anything that day. However, for the second mission in a row, he lost his wingman in the frenzied fighting. As Bong was trying to break up a group of Zeros homing in on a damaged Lightning, Lieutenant Stanley Johnson was hit by a barrage from a zooming Zero. He went down, one of the five P-38s and their fliers lost that day.

We can assume Bong was disturbed by Johnson's loss, by that of Haniotis, too, even though it was typical to have friends and flight mates die in such a dangerous game as the one they were playing. And men performing duty as hazardous as aerial combat became jaded to the carnage. Pilots were lost on almost every mission. But in this case, these men were chosen to fly as Bong's wingmen. Their job was to stick with and help him attack and defend. One definition states that a wingman is "a pilot who supports another pilot in a potentially dangerous flying situation, even if it means giving up an easy kill or putting his own plane and life at risk."

At some point, though, Bong had to wonder if he had been doing something wrong, if anything he had done up there had somehow led to the deaths of two good friends so close together. Or was it simply a quirk of fate? It is likely, though, that if Bong had asked such questions out loud, someone would have reminded him that any man in the squadron would have willingly volunteered to fly wing for him anytime. They knew he had a reputation for not putting his wingman in bad situations, and as previously mentioned, he often rewarded them with credit for kills for which he was most likely primarily responsible.

At any rate, he did not have much time to contemplate the situation. When Dick got back to the base, orders awaited him. He was to report to General Kenney's headquarters ASAP. He showed up in a plain olive drab shirt and pants. That had become the preferred uniform for the men stationed there in the cloyingly humid climate of New Guinea. In truth, they often wore no shirt at all and cut the pants legs off at the knees to try to stay cool. Bong sincerely believed he had dressed up for his audience with the general.

Kenney gave him some static over his attire, insisting he don for the entire trip home a dress uniform with his medals and ribbons arrayed on his chest. Bong admitted he had lost the only dress uniform he had been issued, so the general sent him off to a local tailor to get him set up with the proper duds—something befitting his service branch's top fighter pilot. And he was to have all the ribbons he had earned sewn on as well.

Kenney had good reason for dressing Bong up. He knew the press and the military higher-ups back home would be all over the kid. For many reasons, Bong needed to look like the hero he was.

The farm boy was not even sure what some of the ribbons stood for, so he asked Kenney to explain them to him. Bong insisted he did not want to know so he could brag about them, but just in case somebody along the way should ask.

Bong departed Australia on November 9, 1943, bound for Washington, DC, and a meetup with General Hap Arnold. Bong, who had only turned twenty-three years old a month and a half before, carried with him a letter from Kenney to Arnold. In that letter, Kenney asked that Bong be afforded leave time to "go home, do some hunting, strut his stuff around the hometown, and get some of his mother's home cooking that he was always bragging about." It was not in the letter, but Kenney had also suggested the kid find himself a good Midwestern farm girl while he was Stateside, someone with whom he could eventually settle down and raise a house full of little Bongs. It was neither the first nor the last time the general made such a recommendation to the young officer.

Dick was not due back in New Guinea until February 1, 1944. Meanwhile, the war would just have to go on without him.

He could not have anticipated the reception he was about to receive back in the USA. Nor could he have known that he would soon be able to follow his commander's advice. Like many of his fellow pilots, Dick Bong would soon have a girl's name to paint on the nose of his P-38.

CHAPTER SEVENTEEN

MARGE

There was no way Captain Richard Ira Bong could have been prepared for all that happened to him during his two-month visit home. Not for the heady few days when he was sported around Washington, DC, as a conquering hero, already a favorite of the media but also openly admired by service members of all ranks. Not for all the events held in his honor, not only in his hometown but in New York, Los Angeles, and other imposingly big cities where he would appear. And not for the coincidental series of events back in Wisconsin that would allow him to find and fall in love with the girl he would one day make his wife.

It took him a full week to travel from New Guinea to Washington. He encountered his first herd of newspaper reporters and photographers upon arrival in DC. His every move was choreographed by Army public affairs officers. Such constant attention from the press—and handling by the public affairs guys—would become frustrating.

Dick was a bit nervous about his meeting with General Arnold. The young airman, who showed no fear when sparring with Japanese pilots, was admittedly in awe of Arnold, the aviation hero who had gotten his initial flight training from the Wright Brothers themselves, as well as his lofty position in the wartime chain of command. Arnold was also known to be tough and opinionated, which had caused some controversy during his long career. However, Bong found the general to be warm, welcoming, and genuinely curious, easy to talk to. Just another airplane driver. And the man certainly had plenty of questions for Dick about how the war was going. Throughout the meeting, Arnold seemed honestly interested in hearing Bong's opinions about tactics, equipment, and more.

They conversed for more than an hour; then the general invited him to lunch in the dining room. Once there, Bong looked about and saw no officer below the rank of general. He tried not to be intimidated. He was just happy to be enjoying such a nice meal after all those powdered eggs and milk and "mystery meat" extracted from dented tin cans back in Dobodura.

Halfway through the meal—during which he was interrupted several times by some of those high-ranking officers who seemed to sincerely want to meet and congratulate him—Bong realized that he still had not given Arnold the letter from General Kenney. The one in his coat pocket requesting that the kid be granted that leave time to go back to Poplar and shoot deer. The general smiled as he read the letter and promptly agreed to Kenney's request. He asked Bong when he wanted to leave for the trip home.

"Tonight, by train," Dick immediately shot back, "if that's all right." The weather was miserable, bleak and snowing, and he did not want to take a chance on being delayed any longer, should aircraft be grounded.

Arnold laughed. He would issue the orders right away and have someone check on railway availability from Washington to Wisconsin.

"You better call your folks and tell them you're on the way," he suggested.

It took a couple of days for Bong to get home. In Milwaukee, a pair of resourceful newspaper reporters who had gotten wind of his itinerary met him at the train station. They proposed giving him a lift in their car over the last leg of the trip up to Poplar. In exchange, they wanted Dick to grant them an exclusive interview over the 300 miles and eight hours they would spend on the highway together.

Once they had learned Dick was on the way, reporters and photographers from newspapers and magazines—local and national—began spending time out at the farm with Carl and Dora and Dick's siblings, filing feature stories about the humble beginnings of the farm boy who would come back home for his first visit as a war hero. Now that his arrival was imminent, other newsmen lined the family's driveway to get the first glimpse of the Wisconsin farmer's son turned hero. Carl Bong Jr. later wrote that representatives from media outlets as small as the Superior *Evening Telegram* and as prominent as United Press International and the Associated Press were there to greet his brother and capture the homecoming. So were a military band made up of air cadets from Superior State Teachers College and a gaggle of friends and neighbors.

It was a long, cold wait. Finally, just after one a.m., a car turned off the main road and made its way up the lengthy drive to the Bongs' farmhouse. Mother, father, and all Dick's brothers and sisters pounced on him when he climbed from the car. Flashbulbs popped and reporters yelled questions about "shooting down Japs" and his latest total number of "kills" and how had he managed to become so effective at knocking down all those "Nips."

His mother promptly put an end to all that. She told everyone her boy had endured a long, arduous journey and he needed to get to sleep. He would be home until the end of January. They would have an opportunity to ask him all those questions later.

Bong's answers to those sorts of inquiries remained consistent throughout his time at home. Consistent and characteristically modest.

"I'm just lucky," he told them. "Lots of Japs just happened to get in my way, I guess. I keep shooting and they get in my way somehow." That or similar quotes showed up in articles nationwide, usually accompanied by photos of Dick making a speech, talking to pilot trainees, or preparing to go deer hunting.

But he also shared with his family and friends that he did not especially like to talk about death, of "kills," of him being a "killer," even if he was taking out despised enemy fighters. As did many in the military, he avoided thinking of his adversaries as living, breathing people. Men with families back home awaiting their return. Instead, to him, those were simply Zeros and Oscars he knocked out of the heavens. It was the airplanes that were shooting back at him. He was trained for and dedicated to shooting down those inanimate objects so as not to be shot down himself.

Dick got only a few hours of sleep that first night back in his own bed. Today we would say he had jet lag. His internal clock was badly off-kilter. And besides, he was anxious to visit with his friends as soon as he could. At least those few who were not also off somewhere fighting for their country. He had only one day before deer season opened and he and his dad and brothers could legally go claim some whitetails.

Once they were finally able to take to the woods—thankfully out of reach of reporters and well-intentioned townspeople wanting to shake hands and slap him on the back—they made quite the haul. Carl Sr. took down a ten-point buck early on their first morning. The Bong hunting party—which included brothers, uncles, and cousins—claimed a total of seven bucks over four days. As he had dreamed, Dick Bong would soon have his fill of venison.

He had been away from home for a full two years since his hurried trip back to Poplar in November of 1941 while on leave, but he was still surprised at how much things had changed. One big difference became apparent when he learned about the upcoming homecoming celebration at his alma mater, Superior State. Typically, there would have been a bonfire, a vote for the king and queen, and then a big announcement of the winners at a dance. And, of course, a football game. Not in 1943. Not with so many of Wisconsin's young men off fighting in Europe and the Pacific, training to go there, or already wounded or lost in the conflict. There would be no football team during the war. And no male student available to be voted on and crowned home-coming king.

The previous year's queen, a local girl named Marjorie Vatten-dahl, would be called upon to carry out the duty usually relegated to the homecoming king. She would crown the new queen at a greatly slimmed-down dance. The plan was for this year's king to be chosen from the group of aviation cadets who happened to be home on leave at the time. A youngster not even technically a student at Superior State.

Then someone had a brilliant idea. Hero pilot Richard Bong was home on leave, too, and his picture was in all the papers. He was easily the school's most famous alumnus. Why not invite him to appear at the dance and make the event all the more special? Then the students could have him put the crown on the head of the 1943 homecoming queen. Great idea!

The six-girl committee—including Marjorie Vattendahl—rushed out to the Bong farm to coerce in person the town celeb-rity into being a part of the event at his old school. No luck. Bong was, of course, out hunting. However, his sister Geraldine, then also a Superior State student, agreed it was a fine idea. She promised she would talk to her brother and convince him to accept.

Dick consented. Though sometimes painfully shy, he ended up having a fine time that night. And he shared the stage with Marjorie Vattendahl during the coronation. There was an im-mediate attraction.

After the crowning, though, when girls boldly asked Bong to be their dance partner, he turned them all down. He had to con-fess to them that he might be able to pilot a P-38 at 400 miles per hour, but he did not have a clue about how to dance. That was one thing he had never taken the time to learn to do.

Later, at a favorite local diner of his, he was having a bite to eat with Geraldine and her date. It was by coincidence that Marjorie and a girlfriend came in. When the two girls could not find a vacant table, Dick walked over and invited them to join him and the others. Though they kept getting interrupted by autograph seekers and well-wishers throughout their meal, a spark was struck that evening.

A few days later Dick asked Geraldine for a favor. He wanted her to call up that Vattendahl girl and see if she would go out on a double date with him, Geraldine, and her boyfriend.

Marjorie readily agreed. That would be Marge and Dick's first and last double date. But not their last date.

The two became a regular item, seeing each other throughout his few weeks at home. Or at least anytime Dick was not busy with other commitments or deer hunting. He even took Marge and his mother up in a rented Piper Cub and buzzed both their houses.

However, the Army intended to get as much morale-building, recruiting, and PR value from their handsome hero fighter pilot as they could. That meant Bong had to attend events, make appearances, and sit for media interviews, not only near home but also around the country. He was to help sell war bonds, a typical US savings bond earmarked to help finance the war effort. He would also encourage young men to volunteer for flight training and help convince the general public that the Allies had finally turned around the war in the Pacific despite a discouraging couple of years.

The town of Superior declared January 7 to be "Dick Bong Day" and threw a big party for him. The local American Legion chapter and the Veterans of Foreign Wars pitched another celebration with banners reading "Bonds, Bombs, Bullets, and Bong" draped all around the VFW hall. He helped launch a vessel at Globe Shipbuilding Company in Superior, surrounded by admiring Rosie the Riveters. He was invited to a reception with the governor down in the state capital of Madison. Then he was on an airplane to Los Angeles to be part of a big rally at the Hollywood Bowl, headlined by crooner Bing Crosby. But Richard Bong was the big star of this show. The banner over the stage for the event was an obvious choice: "Bing and Bong!" He had spent the week between Christmas and New Year's in New York City, answering over and over the same questions from reporters and radio commentators, and still dutifully hawking war bonds.

Dick did make it back to Poplar in time to spend New Year's Eve with Marjorie, welcoming in 1944 together. By the time the last week of January approached, it was clear to both Dick and Marge—as he now called her—that they were serious about each other and wanted a future together. But it was a complicated situation. Dick knew what the odds against him were out there. He did not want to leave Marge a widow with a legacy of less than two distracted months together.

During his time at home, he had met with the widow of his recently lost wingman, Stanley Johnson. She had coincidentally come to Superior to visit with some friends, saw all the press about Dick Bong being just down the road, and reached out to him. Talking with her about her husband's last minutes of life had a strong effect on Dick and, ultimately, his and Marge's plans for marriage.

He told Marge in no uncertain terms that he wanted to marry her. But they would have to wait until he was back from the war for good. She understood. And agreed. She would pray hard that peace would come before long. That they could then start their life and family together.

Before he left Poplar, Dick had one more chore to do. He asked Marge to send him a good picture of herself. One he could keep in his wallet and show off to all his buddies back in New Guinea. One he could place in the cockpit, on the instrument panel of his fighter.

He did not tell her that he also intended to enlarge the photo and attach it to the left side of the nose of his P-38, just above the name "Marge" written in large bold script. It was a special spot, just behind those lethal guns, and just ahead of those twenty-one small "Rising Sun" flag emblems that represented his accomplishments so far in the war.

And now he had a new reason to want to help bring it to a speedy end.

CHAPTER EIGHTEEN

"THE FLYING CIRCUS"

Geneeral George Churchill Kenney had mixed feelings about the fervid competition among his best fighter pilots to reach the top of the count of the most combat kills. On the one hand, several of them—relative newcomers like Lieutenant Tommy McGuire, Captain James Watkins, and Major Gerald Johnson—were showing their skill and determination. They were usually claiming two or three enemy planes shot down every time they experienced serious aerial fighting. But on the other hand, and despite how their remarkable success was contributing to the war effort, he did not want such passionate competition to compel them to take undue risks in an effort to light up the scoreboard.

By the time Dick Bong went home for Christmas 1943, he was the man to beat, despite his reluctance to be a part of the contest. Neel Kearby was still the closest competitor to Bong when Dick returned to the fray in February 1944, now with his picture of Marge on the nacelle of his P-38. Kearby was one of the ones Kenney was most nervous about taking risks for another notch on his gunstock. Just before Bong reported back to Dobo, the general had a serious conversation with Kearby about his concerns. Kenney later wrote, "Neel . . . was credited with twenty victories, one behind Captain Dick Bong, who was due back in a few days. I told Kearby not to engage in a race with that cool little Scandinavian boy. Bong didn't care who was high man. He would never be in a race, and I didn't want Kearby to press his luck and take too many chances for the sake of having his name first on the scoreboard."

Kenney told Kearby he was going to send him off for some rest. Kearby resisted. He responded that he wanted to remain in the game just a bit longer, until he had a nice, even fifty kills.

Fifty! Kenney had to admire the pilot's enthusiasm, but such swagger also caused him even more concern. Still, the general reluctantly agreed to allow him to fly, but only for another month or so. Then, fifty kills or not, he was to be sent Stateside for a while to rest, do PR, and sell war bonds—all with the same bravado with which he attacked enemy aircraft.

Kearby, still flying his P-47 Thunderbolt fighter, continued his hot streak, briefly tying Bong for kills. The Texan and Medal of Honor recipient had already been targeted by the war correspondents as the pilot most likely to eclipse the kid. That earned Kearby plenty of ink. When the movie actor John Wayne visited the area, it was Kearby that the USAAF and reporters made sure was photographed shaking hands with "Duke."

The media happily fanned the flames of competition between Kearby and Bong. Such a rivalry made for good copy and grand headlines. Up to that point in the war, the South Pacific was still playing second fiddle in the consciousness of not only military leaders but also the press and even the general public back home. Reporters covering the Pacific War needed a good angle to get their stories toward the front and above the fold in the daily papers. The race among these charismatic young fighter pilots to be America's top ace gave them just that.

General Kenney did not object. And it was one of the reasons he had allowed Kearby to continue to fly missions even as he worried that the Texan might be pushing too hard. Such hero stories in the newspapers and on the radio back home attracted the attention of not only the general's bosses but also politicians who could pressure the Army to give him what he needed to win the war. If that press hastened the shipment of a bunch of P-38s or the assignment of more new pilots to the Pacific instead of to Europe, then the ace competition would be worth it. So long as nobody got hurt in the process, of course.

While we can never be sure if Neel Kearby was pressing his luck at the time or not, we do know his plane went down and he was lost about a month later in a fiery crash over Wewak. Lost while once again trailing Dick Bong, who had picked up right where he left off before going home to shoot deer instead of enemy airplanes.

George Kenney's gamble had failed. Kearby's death was front-page news back home. The loss of a Medal of Honor recipient and top ace fighter pilot was big news, of course.

There were others chasing Bong, too, but it seemed that every time they approached his total, they also dropped out of the race for one reason or another. Sometimes tragically. With sixteen tallies, Major George Welch—one of the two pilots who had famously gotten airborne during the sneak attack on Pearl Harbor in December 1941 and shot down enemy planes—had suffered from bouts of malaria and eventually had to resign from the USAAF. He went back to the US to become a civilian test pilot for North American Aviation. His service in the Pacific was over.

Two other potential challengers died in combat while Dick Bong was on leave in Wisconsin. Captain Daniel Roberts—nicknamed the "Quiet Ace" by the press because he did not drink or swear—had established a hefty total. He collected sixteen credited kills—later reduced to fourteen—in less than three months of action. But then he was lost November 9 when his P-38 collided with another Lightning while engaged in a dogfight with a Ki-43 Oscar.

Another top ace, Major Edward Cragg, had fifteen confirmed kills when he was shot down the day after Christmas 1943. Cragg was commander of the 80th Fighter Squadron at the time he went missing over New Britain. He had been responsible for their colorful nickname, the "Headhunters," and had commissioned a former Walt Disney Studios artist to design their distinctive squadron patch.

Major Tommy Lynch was another ace who was challenging Bong for the position at the top of the board. The same Tommy Lynch for whom Bong had flown as wingman in some hot action back in December of 1942. Kenney had sent Lynch home for some well-deserved leave—for him it was thirty days—in October of 1943. At the time, he had eighteen verified kills on his record and appeared to be the most likely to catch and surpass Dick Bong. The Eagle Scout and chemical engineering grad from the University of Pittsburgh had taken advantage of his time back home to marry his girlfriend from college, Rosemary. Then, when he got back to New Guinea, Lynch found himself— along with fellow ace Dick Bong—in an unusual situation, a relatively new assignment structure that the AAF felt would allow these top pilots to do what they did but even better.

The commander of the Fifth Fighter Command, General Paul Wurtsmith, informed Lynch and Bong that they were no longer a part of their previous unit at Dobodura. Lynch was to be reassigned as Wurtsmith's operative officer and Dick was to become Lynch's assistant.

Both pilots immediately objected. They had no interest in any mundane, ground-based desk jobs. They were combat fighter pilots. And damn good ones. Nobody had ever shot down an Oscar or a Zero from behind a desk.

Wurtsmith grinned, held up a hand, and explained that Bong and Lynch would no longer be part of a specific combat squadron. They would still have command responsibilities, but they would now have the freedom to pick the units with which they flew and the missions of which they would be a part. And such choices could be last-minute and completely up to Lynch and Bong, so long as the chosen unit's commander agreed.

Lynch and Bong would be freelancers. The two of them could fly together as a team or they could butt right into any other squadron anywhere within the Fifth at any time.

The general pointed out that the new assignment policy was already underway with some of the other top pilots. While the two of them had been on leave, several others—including Neel

Kearby—had been similarly reallocated. It was working well for everybody but the Empire of Japan.

One minor restriction remained, though. Along with their new responsibilities, there would also be a requirement to perform routine staff duties. And those necessarily came first.

Wurtsmith might have winked when he explained that lone stipulation to Bong and Lynch. Both men knew there would not likely be enough paperwork to deter them from getting back into the skies and doing all the damage they could.

There was another underlying reason for the unusual assignment policy for Bong, Lynch, and the others. It had once again become frustratingly difficult to get new P-38s and the spare parts to keep the older ones flying. By this time, the number of all-Lightning squadrons had necessarily been reduced, too. While Wurtsmith could have crowbarred his top two pilots into one of the remaining P-38 groups, he instead came up with the idea of making them part of his staff. That meant he would have them wherever they felt like going in the air. They were now part of any P-38 squadron they chose to fly with.

The new assignment also came with new equipment. The USAAF wanted these freelancers to have the best, most advanced airplanes. Both Lynch and Bong would now fly the latest, the P-38J variant. It offered an engine cooling system less vulnerable to damage during air-to-air combat. Larger fuel tanks gave it even more range. And there was a specially designed flap installed on the wings behind the engines that gave this latest version of the Lightning much greater speed and stability when making especially steep dives.

However, the most noticeable change was that the aircraft's metal skins were no longer painted in drab green and gray camouflage colors. Such a concealment paint job helped when Japanese air attacks on bases were so common. That made the aircraft less visible parked on the ground, but the masking coloration had been no help in the sky. If anything, the dark green stood out more against clouds. Now the new Lightnings came off the assembly line with a bright, shiny, unpainted metal surface, broken only by the usual decals and stenciled model and serial numbers. The difference in visibility in the air was negligible, but the new no-camouflage look made the planes lighter and as much as twenty miles per hour faster.

The pilots decided the new look gave the Lightnings an even more menacing and distinctive appearance as the planes brilliantly flashed about in the tropical sunlight during midair combat. Like flashes of lightning!

Of course, the first thing Dick Bong did was to ask the squadron's mapping unit to enlarge the picture of Marge Vattendahl she had sent him. He then glued it to his plane's nose, just as so many other pilots had done. They generally preferred risqué cartoons of half-clad women or of fierce, snarling animals. Not Dick Bong.

He had been patiently waiting for just the right name and image and had so far not put anything on the planes he flew. Of course, since the picture was glued on, not painted, it soon faded away because of the speeds at and weather conditions in which he flew. But he kept replacing it—the picture was her Superior State college graduation portrait and certainly not salacious in any way—every time her lovely smile began to dim.

He also modified his new ride by including some touches of bright red paint to several spots, including the tips of the propellers, on the otherwise silvery airplane. Then, with the addition of the small Japanese flags representing each of his kills to date, he felt he had himself a true "hot rod." (Some fighter pilots refused to put the small rising-sun flags on their birds. They believed such a display of their prowess made them a more desirable target for enemy fighters.)

Interestingly, Marge Vattendahl learned how Dick had used her photo in a roundabout way. She assumed he carried it in his wallet or put it on the instrument panel of his plane, as he had told her he would do when he requested it. But then the military newspaper, *Stars and Stripes*, sent a reporter and photographer out to interview Dick. They wanted a picture of him standing next to his P-38 to accompany the article. That image clearly showed Marge's beautiful smiling face and her name. When reporters back in the States saw the photo, they scrambled to find ace pilot Dick Bong's girl. That was the first time Marge fully realized she was dating a celebrity. And that the media would be a real nuisance to her from then on.

Dick did not help matters when he later shared with another reporter that, once Marge learned of her picture being on his airplane, he had told her, "It's true. And you are now the most shot-at girl in the Southwest Pacific."

Tommy Lynch and Dick Bong soon confirmed their pick-your-mission assignment would pay dividends. On February 10, with a randomly chosen unit, they were flying together, Bong as Lynch's wingman. They spotted a Ki-48 "Lily" light bomber west of Wewak. Lynch promptly shot him down and the two aces were long gone before the Japanese at the nearby base could scramble planes and get them airborne to try to intercept the sharp-shooting duo.

On the fifteenth, the two joined elements of the 80th Fighter Squadron to help escort bombers to New Ireland, beyond New Britain but dangerously near Rabaul. The mission went smoothly, though. Bombs fell on prime targets. Then they all turned back toward home. That was when Bong spotted a lone Ki-61 Tony fighter. This time Dick was flying lead and dived on the target, coming at him from out of the sun, surprising the enemy warplane pilot. *Marge* was just over half a football field's distance away when Bong opened fire, knocking the target out of the sky and into the sea 10,000 feet below.

Only two days later, word came of a transport aircraft carrying a group of high-ranking Japanese staff officers that had left from Rabaul headed to Wewak. It was to be an inspection trip but also an effort to boost morale at the once-dominant facility. Bong and Lynch—now dubbed by General Wurtsmith and their fellow pilots as the "Flying Circus"—accepted the job and rushed to take off.*

Bong and Lynch had no idea if they could get to Wewak in time to greet the planeload of dignitaries. It would be tight. They flew at top speed from where they were then based, the

---

* The nickname Flying Circus had been used by some elements of the German Army Air Service in World War I. Eddie Rickenbacker had titled his memoir *Fighting the Flying Circus*. It would later be claimed by the US Army Air Forces 380th Bomb Group in the Southwest Pacific. The term has generally been defined as an organized group of pilots engaged in public exhibition flying and applied mostly to the early barnstormers who flew aerobatics in air shows between the wars.

newly constructed aerodrome at Nadzab, twenty-five miles up the Markham River from the recently captured-and-controlled Lae. They made it to Wewak just as the enemy transport landed and was taxiing to the safety of a hangar. Lynch realized that, in the rush to get into the air, his gunsights had not been installed. He would be firing blind. He informed Bong the target was his.

Without hesitation, Bong took the shot, and the plane was promptly ablaze. Then, as Dick pulled up and looked back to see if he needed to come around and shoot again, the target exploded spectacularly.

Just for good measure, the two buddies machine-gunned a group of what appeared to be about a hundred Japanese who were there waiting to meet the plane's very important passengers. It would later be confirmed that the plane Bong annihilated carried a major general, a brigadier general, and an assortment of key high-ranking staff officers.

However, there would be no addition to Dick's score for destroying the enemy transport, even though he had every opportunity to claim it. The plane was on the ground, still taxiing, when he hit it. Not in the air. Some air forces counted in a pilot's total any plane he destroyed, no matter where it was or what it was doing at the time. This was not the policy of the USAAF in the Southwest Pacific. Had Bong and Lynch shown up at Wewak a mere three minutes earlier and had Dick gotten the same results, it would have been his twenty-third score.

Kenney argued with Bong about the specifics of the attack. He tried to convince the young pilot that the transport could possibly have been an inch or two off the runway and technically still in flight. Bong merely needed to say that in his incident report and nobody would take issue. Lynch agreed to back up whatever Bong's testimony was. But the kid refused to exaggerate or even hazard a guess. He even wrote in the official report that the plane had stopped rolling at the very moment when he pounded it.

No way it was still flying. No way he would state anything to the contrary.

That hit would have held some importance in the race of the aces. At the time, Neel Kearby had just eliminated two of the empire's best fighter planes and was now temporarily tied with Bong. And all involved were quite aware that Eddie Rickenbacker's World War I record would surely soon be reached and broken. Kenney's promised case of Scotch (and, assumedly, Rickenbacker's offer of another case) would almost certainly go to either Neel Kearby, Tommy Lynch, or Dick Bong. Nobody flying for the USAAF in Europe or there in the Southwest Pacific was anywhere within hailing distance of the scores of those three top guns.

Kenney, who admitted he had not imagined he would ever have to pay off on his impromptu offer, was now more than willing to pony up and properly salute his top ace when the record inevitably fell.

And it did not matter at all to the general which one of his three boys made that happen.

CHAPTER NINETEEN

COKE AND BEDSHEETS

As of March 5, 1944, when Neel Kearby's P-47 Thunderbolt plunged straight down into the jungle near Wewak, the race for the case of fine Scotch for beating Eddie Rickenbacker's World War I record was effectively down to two pilots. And while one of them could not have cared less about such things, the other was still openly gung ho and regularly checking scores. Dick Bong and Tommy Lynch were flying together as part of a fighter sweep over New Guinea the same day Kearby went down, and they both bagged two enemy planes on that run. Bong claimed a couple of light bombers and Lynch shot down another bomber and a fighter. That gave Bong twenty-four confirmed and Lynch twenty-one, even as Neel Kearby's count would tragically and forever remain at twenty-two.

It seemed that the ace who would break Rickenbacker's record was often flying wingman for the other contender. Kearby's loss dimmed spirits a bit, but the competition helped take everyone's mind off the harsh realities of war.

Bets were placed. Fellow pilots aligned behind their favorite and cheered him on. Reporters watched the updates with even greater interest. What a great story! Since the top two contenders so often flew missions together, the loser would likely be called upon to bear witness to confirm the winner's twenty-seventh kill. Then, with that significant barrier broken, they could all keep score to see which of the two—or which other hard charger now only a few kills behind but coming on strong—would ultimately be the war's top fighter pilot.

Bong and Lynch were once again flying as teammates on the morning of March 9, sortieing by themselves on a relatively mundane mission. The Allies had been pummeling an enemy airfield at Tadji, New Guinea, about ninety miles northwest of Wewak and also located on the northern coast. Plans were well underway for a ground assault on the area in April as part of Operation Persecution, a mission to simultaneously try to take Tadji and the port of Hollandia, even farther up to the northwest. Once they were captured and secure, the Army would have operational bases even closer to the Philippines.

This day, though, the Army simply needed somebody to fly over and see if the reported damage to the long runway at Tadji was as severe as the bomber crews believed. If so, they could be sure that there would be no air support coming from there to defend it, Hollandia, and the remaining enemy-controlled territory on New Guinea.

The two pilots volunteered for this routine assignment in the hopes they would encounter enemy fighters to engage. No luck. There were none. The sky was filled only with puffy clouds and native birds.

They did determine through a couple of low-level flyovers that the Japanese had so far not patched up any of the huge bomb craters at Tadji. That made the runway useless. Their assignment done, and with most of their fuel and all of their ammunition remaining, Bong and Lynch decided they would scout around for other potential targets. It took only a quick pivot to the north to put them out over where the waters of the Bismarck Sea mingled with those of the Pacific Ocean. Maybe they would find an enemy ship or two, something worthy of their 20mm cannon shells. Possibly supply ships headed for Tadji or Hollandia.

Sure enough, only a few miles offshore, they spied a small convoy. It included a Japanese corvette, the smallest vessel typically dubbed a warship, lesser in size than a frigate and often used by the enemy to escort reduced and slower convoys. This one was doing just that, protecting two sailing vessels plying their way westward. Though corvettes were less sizable ships, they did typically carry lethal weaponry. That alone made the vessel an attractive target for the two aces. And the luggers it protected were likely hauling supplies for ground troops in the area—troops who in a few weeks would be trying to repulse Operation Persecution or the attempt to claim the port of Hollandia.

Bong and Lynch independently decided the .50-caliber machine guns would be better suited to sink the corvette and give them something to show for this day's run. Even if it did not feed the frenzy around their air combat kill totals. The two men took turns diving on the vessel, dodging its toxic counterfire at near-wave-top level, then pulling up to circle around and attack again.

They were inflicting damage on the vessel. It was only a matter of time before they sank her and turned their attention and bullets to the other, less well-armed ships.

But then, looking back over his shoulder, Bong saw Lynch's plane suddenly break off his dive, likely only a thousand feet or so above the sea. He then made a ragged turn away from the corvette, back toward the distant shoreline. Smoke was pouring from his left engine. At that altitude, Lynch could be in serious trouble.

Bong broke off his own dive and followed his friend. If Tommy had to bail out, it would be important for a quick and successful rescue if Bong was able to see exactly where his wingman's parachute settled down among the dense foliage.

But then the propeller on the damaged engine suddenly flew right off. So did much of the nose of the Lightning. Then away went the cockpit canopy. The plane was coming apart and was now even more swallowed up by bright red flames.

"Get out, Tommy!" Bong yelled into his radio microphone. "You're low!"

But Dick knew that Lynch was coming out now, whether he wanted to or not. That is, if he was not badly hurt.

But even if he could manage to unbuckle himself and deploy his parachute as his airplane flew apart, he was likely much too close to the ground for it to do him much good. As Bong watched, he thought he saw his buddy emerge from what was left of his plane and tumble away from the wreckage. But there was no parachute trailing out above him, catching air.

It could have been Lynch. It could have been just another piece of his airplane.

As Dick drew even closer, the damaged plane abruptly exploded, disintegrating. There was still no sure sign of Tommy Lynch. Or a parachute.

Dick circled, trying to catch a glimpse of his friend. Of his 'chute. Nothing. Below, on the ground, there were only columns of black smoke in the jungle beyond the beach where larger pieces of Lynch's plane had hit the ground and continued to burn.

Bong flew around for a bit, trying to see some sign that Tommy had miraculously survived the crash. There was nothing to offer hope.

Dick considered going back out to seek revenge against the corvette, but he was now marginal on fuel. He finally relented and headed back to Nadzab to report the incident.

He no longer had a wingman for what remained of that day's mission.

When General Kenney got word of the loss of a second one of his star pilots in less than a week, he was consumed with renewed worries about the mental state of his top gun. Not only had Dick Bong lost two fellow pilots with whom he had flown many missions. He had also witnessed the death of the latest one. An especially terrible death.

"I was afraid that seeing Tommy go that way might affect his nerve," the general would later recall. "So, I ordered him down to Brisbane to ferry a new plane back to [Nadzab]. I sent a message to the depot commander [in Brisbane] that if the airplane he was going after was ready to fly before another couple of weeks I would demote him at least two pay grades."

It was Kenney's way of sneakily giving Bong two weeks of leave away from the death and destruction of the war. He figured that would allow the kid time to deal with the horrific loss of his friend. It was true that Dick had flown a couple of routine missions after Lynch's crash and before he received his orders to go to Brisbane without incident, and the young man had shown no signs of stress or depression. What most called "shell shock."

Even so, Kenney stuck to his guns. The top-scoring ace in World War II so far would now be relegated to sitting on the beach for a couple of weeks—lathered up with plenty of sunscreen, enjoying real meals, and sleeping ten to twelve hours a day in a comfortable bed. Only then would he be allowed to play deliveryman with the new warplane.

Kenney was away for a few days, but when he returned to his headquarters in Brisbane, he made it a point to meet up with Bong, mostly to try to ascertain his mental state. The "Scandinavian" appeared to be just fine. The kid seemed to have the ability to shut out emotional trauma that would have taken down most other men. Yes, he was frustrated that it was taking so long to get the newly assembled plane ready to fly to Nadzab. But for the most part he was just bored, ready to go back to work.

Kenney learned Dick had kept busy during his exile. He had not spent all his time on the beach or napping. He had found a way to push through military bureaucracy and obtain ration coupons to buy a nice set of sheets for the lumpy mattress on his Army cot. He had also acquired four cases of fresh Coca-Cola, his favorite beverage, in glass bottles, a luxury unlikely to be found up there on the northern shore of New Guinea.

But there was one problem with that prize. There was no room for the soda pop on the plane he was to ferry home. So Dick worked with a member of the assembly team putting the plane together out at the depot. He designed and helped the team attach a special rigging beneath each wing, a contraption big enough to hold the cases of Coke yet not interfere with the craft's airworthiness.

Kenney deduced that Bong was okay, ready to go back to work. And God knew he and the USAAF needed the sharpshooter in the cockpit of a P-38. But before sending him back to the war, he took his young pilot over for a visit with General MacArthur. The two proven warriors seemed impressed with each other. Both MacArthur and Kenney strongly suggested to Bong that he avoid strafing runs in the future—action such as the attack that had claimed the life of Tommy Lynch. He should especially avoid targets that were more than able to shoot back at him with considerable accuracy. Instead, they told Bong, he should engage the enemy in the sky, where he and his P-38 had some advantage.

Then, with no other excuses to hold Bong out of the fray, Kenney called up the commander at the depot and told him to go ahead and allow the new plane, its pilot, and its cargo of bedsheets and Coke to fly away.

CHAPTER TWENTY

"I HAD TO SHOOT THEM DOWN"

D ick Bong took the high-level advice to heart and did little if any strafing over the next six weeks. After all, there were plenty of airborne targets buzzing all about as he and the other pilots flew multiple missions in support of the assault on Hollandia and the few remaining enemy installations along the northern shores of New Guinea. There was no cause to look for targets on the ground.

One problem: While Dick was biding his time in Australia, waiting to ferry that airplane back to Nadzab, another pilot, Lieutenant Tom Malone, had borrowed *Marge* to conduct reconnaissance flights over the interior of the island. He ran into intense turbulence over the high mountain peaks, which led to severe mechanical issues, and he had no choice but to bail out. Malone was not hurt. He was picked up by Allied troops and returned to the base. However, Bong's P-38 with his girlfriend's picture on the nose was lost, likely forever. It went down in some of the world's thickest jungle, soon to be swallowed up by vegetation, where it would rust away. It will likely never be found.

Before he even had a chance to put Marge's picture on his next plane, a borrowed Lightning, Bong was back in the sky and adding to his score. On April 3, flying as part of the 432nd Fighter Squadron of the 475th Fighter Group, he found himself in a frenzied air battle over Hollandia. The Allies sent a huge force of more than 300 aircraft, escorted by Bong and a herd of P-38s, to pulverize targets in preparation for taking the strategically important areas later in the month.

The enemy responded to all the attackers with a group of hastily scrambled fighters. Bong fired on several approaching Oscars but missed. He had lately been complaining to his superiors— even as he led the league in hits—that he was not really a good shot at all. All those high scores he had gotten during gunnery training at Luke Field were exaggerated. Now his success came from getting too close to targets to miss. He also had a knack for anticipating the maneuvers of enemy pilots, placing his own P-38 in precisely the best spot to get off a lethal shot. That covered for what he felt was a lack of training in how to properly shoot. He was a good shot with a deer rifle. Shooting at a zooming target while traveling at close to 400 miles per hour was a different thing altogether. And Dick Bong was convinced it was a learned skill. He told everyone who would listen, including General Kenney, that he needed some more gunnery training.

Getting close before opening fire was exactly what happened that morning, and it allowed Dick to claim shoot-down number twenty-five. The very skillful Oscar pilot—the Allies were seeing fewer of those these days as the empire was losing fliers faster than they could be conscripted and trained—had managed to evade two other P-38s with some mighty fancy flying. The Japanese craft had suffered only minor damage, and the airman could soon inflict some serious destruction of his own if nobody took him out.

That was when Dick Bong sensed where the enemy plane was about to be in the crowded sky. He manipulated his borrowed fighter to put it right on the Ki-43's tail. The Oscar pilot likely never saw Bong, who promptly and from point-blank range delivered a knockdown punch.

The Lightning pilots of the 475th claimed more than two dozen enemy fighters that day, but it was Bong's single kill that everybody was talking about. One more would tie the legendary Rickenbacker, the greatest American fighter ace of all time. Never mind that Marine Corps pilot Joe Foss had gotten his twenty-sixth credited kill two months before over Guadalcanal. Foss had been sent home to receive the Medal of Honor but also to avoid the possibility of such a hero being killed in action. Too late for Neel Kearby, it had become common practice by this time not to send Medal of Honor recipients back into combat, air, sea, or land. And for that very reason. Foss also suffered from bouts of malaria, as did many Americans stationed in the tropics.*

---

*The colorful Foss, known as "Smokey Joe," would later return to the Southwest Pacific but would not fly any more combat missions. After the war, he went on to be elected governor of South Dakota, was commissioner of the American Football League before its merger with the NFL, was host of the network TV show *American Sportsman*, became president of the National Rifle Association, and was a successful businessman, but he would forever be tied with Eddie Rickenbacker as an ace fighter pilot.

Someone mentioned to Dick Bong that the USAAF would likely send him home, too, once he broke the Rickenbacker record. He responded that he would not object to such a thing. He missed his family and was anxious to see Marge again, too. According to his brother, Dick wrote home after the April 3 action, saying, "They tell me that if I get twenty-seven confirmed they will send me home so fast I won't know what hit me. Good idea, I think." He also mentioned in the same letter that he was probably going to ask Marge to marry him if he broke the record and got to spend leave time in Poplar. He completed that part of his letter with the same opinion: "Good idea, I think."

That trip home became a probability on April 12, 1944. This time, he flew another borrowed Lightning as part of an even bigger group of bombers and P-38 escorts—200 of the former, sixty of the latter—bound for targets stretching from Hollandia all the way back to the east to near Wewak. His position in the formation that morning was one usually loathed by fighter pilots, that of "tail-end Charlie," bringing up the rear. Somebody had to be last in line. Enemy pilots from Europe to the Pacific often chose that unfortunate guy as their first target because they could slip up on him, attacking before anyone else in the formation even knew they were there. It was an almost guaranteed kill.

Dick Bong, though, liked being tail-end Charlie. He told others that it meant he would be the first to engage, that he could quickly switch from being the prey to becoming the predator. He just had to be sure he was always aware, watching his "six," baiting his attackers, and then shooting them before they shot him.

Sure enough, as they approached the coast near Hollandia, he was one of the first to see a bunch of Oscars and Tonys coming to greet them. Bong picked out an Oscar and chased the enemy plane into a cloud. But Dick was already close enough to shoot and let loose on the fleeing target just as he disappeared. Then, when Bong broke through the bottom of the rain cloud, he saw the Oscar was on fire and breaking apart. It crashed hard into the bay below. One of his squadron mates, passing nearby, saw the whole thing.

Number twenty-six was downed and duly witnessed.

But the battle was hardly over. Back to altitude, Bong spied a couple of enemy fighters trying to flee the mayhem. He gave chase. When he sensed he was close enough not to miss, he sprayed one of the planes with .50-caliber bullets. It began to smoke and fly erratically. He gave the other target a quick burst and it, too, was soon smoking badly. Then both of the enemy birds disappeared into another thick cloud.

Bong did not pursue. They were likely goners, whether he could ever claim them or not. Time, fuel, and ammo were limited quantities. And there were more targets zooming around above him.

Next thing he saw was an Oscar on the tail of another Lightning, giving chase and shooting. With a few quick moves on Bong's part, it became an easy shot for him. He hit the plane's vulnerable engine compartment. It gushed metal parts and fire as it abruptly nosed down. Bong circled and watched it plunge into the sea far below.

Then, directly in front of and a few hundred feet below him, another Oscar appeared. Dick dived on it and chased it all the way down to the deck, maybe ten feet above the wave tops. Again, when he felt he was close enough, he fired a burst that clearly hit the target's left wing, the cockpit area—including the unprotected pilot—and the engine. The resulting damage caused the plane to involuntarily bank hard to its left, and what remained of the mangled wing dipped into the water. That sent the aircraft tumbling, after which it struck a coral formation just beneath the waves and then crashed hard into the green water. It quickly disappeared. By the time Dick had zipped past, turned, and come back for a look, there were only a few pieces of floating junk and an oil slick where the Oscar had so violently gone down.

Bong did chase another enemy fighter after that but was unable to get close enough to launch a meaningful shot. Even with all the damage he had done that day, that last target getting away left Bong frustrated. He had not been confident about how accurately he could fire from that distance and take down the Nakajima Ki-43. The missed opportunity bothered him.

When he returned to Nadzab that night and began writing up his incident report, Bong would initially claim three kills. That would have given him a total of twenty-eight. But he soon learned that only two of them would count. Those were the only ones that other pilots had witnessed. Since he was in a borrowed plane, it had not been loaded with film for its gun camera before Dick jumped in it and took off.

The day's third victim, the one about which he was most sure, was the Oscar he had chased all the way down to the water. The one he had sent tumbling into the coral before it sank into Tanahmerah Bay.

But again, no witness, no film, no confirmation.

Oh, well. He was not in this for the math. He was proud he

had exceeded the score of America's top ace. That should be enough to get him a ticket home for a few weeks. Then he could come back and add to the tally. And, of course, make a contribution to ending the war.

The record breaker meant far more to General Kenney, the media, and the folks back in the US than it did to Richard Bong. Though an Army pilot in Europe would also break Rickenbacker's record a month later, Kenney made sure everyone knew it was one of his boys who had gotten there first. When Bong got his twenty-sixth, the general promoted him to the rank of major, effective April 12. That just happened to be the day he broke the existing record. Headlines back home crowed about America's new ace of aces, young Richard Bong of Wisconsin. The NBC Radio Network cobbled together limited existing technology, including shortwave radio, to do a live broadcast featuring Rickenbacker and Bong speaking to each other from different sides of the planet. Or, truthfully, reading from scripts prepared by the network's news writers and the military. That gave the conversation a very stilted, rehearsed sound, but it still reached a wide listening audience.

Back home, Bong's dad, mother, and siblings in Poplar were again hounded by reporters and newsreel photographers. Journalists descended on Superior State Teachers College, trying to get comments from and pictures of Marge Vattendahl. Some even invaded classrooms where she was continuing her studies and at East High School, where she was doing her practice teaching.

"I was called out of classes because some reporter wanted to know this and that," she later wrote. "Shots were taken of me in the classroom . . . and at our campus hangout, the Coffee Shop."

Army Air Forces public relations specialists tried to help channel the intense interest even as they fanned the flames and kept it going. They would get as much mileage as they could from the record breaker, all to sell bonds, help morale, and entice recruits to come learn to fly and fight for the Army. Not necessarily for the Navy.

A week after the mission, Dick wrote home, saying, "I've heard you are having trouble with the reporters back there. I'm certainly having my troubles with them. I broke the record and by so doing procured for myself a lot of trouble. I suppose Marge is catching hell, too. I wasn't thinking far enough ahead or I would not have put her picture on my airplane and she could have lived in peace."

Dick ended that letter in his usual modest way: "I didn't figure on breaking the record, but they got in front of me so I had to shoot them down."

Bong received a rather cautionary special-delivery letter of congratulations from Rickenbacker, by way of General Kenney.

"I . . . hope you will double or treble this number," the World War I hero offered. "But in trying, use the same calculating techniques that have brought you results to date, for we will need your kind back home after this war is over. My promise of a case of Scotch still holds. So be on the lookout for it."

That whole case-of-Scotch controversy was rekindled when Bong broke Rickenbacker's record. Some still felt Allied warriors should be spending their time fighting Nazis and Nips, not kicking back, getting lit. Temperance organizations and religious groups revolted, demanding no alcohol incentives be offered to America's young fighting men.

Bong did not really dwell much on the hullabaloo. When the case from Rickenbacker showed up—he had received scores of offers from breweries and bars willing to donate the Scotch, mostly in exchange for publicity for having done so—and General Kenney provided his promised case, Dick simply hosted a party and invited every officer, pilot, support person, construction team member, and soldier within miles of Nadzab. Two cases of Scotch turned out to be enough for only a glass or two per attendee. Not enough for anybody to "get lit."

General Hap Arnold had offered his own congrats by shipping out to Bong several cases of soda pop.

"I understand you prefer this type of refreshment to the others," he wrote. "You thoroughly deserve to have the kind you want. The Army Air Forces are proud of you and your splendid record. Congratulations!"

When the media were reminded that General Douglas MacArthur had initially added a case of champagne to the bounty for any pilot who broke the twenty-six-kill mark, he quickly distanced himself from the controversy. His people issued a statement saying liquor was not an appropriate reward, though he did have "the highest admiration for Major Bong's skill and gallantry."

Bong quickly grew weary of all the media attention. After reporters staged a card game with him, convincing him to sit in with them around a table in Port Moresby, the scribes penned stories comparing the daring way the young man played poker with how he flew his P-38 into combat against the Japanese. Other journalists descended on the various air bases around the big island, seeking from his fellow pilots any anecdotes or personal details about the hero Bong.

Photographers excitedly proposed shooting pictures of Bong again standing next to his fighter plane, the one with the picture of Marge Vattendahl on the nacelle. Maybe of him adding the twenty-seventh flag decal. Or sitting in the cockpit as if he were ready to fly off and shoot down still more enemy planes. Then they were disappointed to learn that airplane was no more. It was in the jungle halfway up the flank of one of the peaks of the Stanley Mountains, likely already covered with vines. But USAAF public affairs was only too willing to re-create that artwork on another P-38. One Dick Bong had never piloted. And no one mentioned that the lost Lightning with the original likeness of Miss Vattendahl had been flown by Bong only while he was collecting four of the twenty-seven. If details did not make good copy or serve the USAAF's preferred publicity purposes, they were conveniently ignored.

Unbeknownst to Dick Bong, a few days after the mission during which the record fell, George Kenney had received a cryptic note bearing the signature of General Hap Arnold.

It read, "Concern is expressed over the high loss rate of fighter pilots who have shot down many enemy aircraft. Your comments are requested concerning the desirability of restricting from action combat flying or return to United States of this type personnel. A case in point is [Major] Bong, who is credited with twenty-seven enemy aircraft. Only very recently we have lost the invaluable services of Colonels Kearby and Lynch."

General Kenney, of course, had already decided to do just that.

A hero pilot could do worlds of good on the PR circuit. And it also gave him a break from the stress of flying those highly dangerous missions. Kenney doubted that not being able to add to his score right away would concern Bong. Besides, the next closest to him now was Tommy McGuire, with twenty confirmed. However, he was currently in the middle of a dry spell. And besides, Bong had been lobbying not so subtly for a while now to be sent Stateside to undergo gunnery training so he could be even more effective.

Still, Kenney hated to lose one of his most valuable warriors at such a critical time in the war, even if only for a month or so. But now even the big boss wanted it to be so.

Reluctantly, the general wired Arnold that he had indeed removed Major Bong from combat duty. He was sending Bong home for a couple of weeks of leave, and then the airman was to go to aerial gunnery school. That would be at Foster Field, Matagorda County, Texas, on the Gulf of Mexico. Once his training was completed there, Bong was to return to New Guinea, where he would teach other fighter pilots what he had learned.

Kenney believed many of his pilots—including some of his best ones—had been trained how to shoot plane to plane when such teaching was not yet fully developed. Weapons and airplanes had changed considerably in three years of fighting. There was value in making each of his fighter pilots even more skilled as gunners. Even so, it seemed odd to be sending the best air warrior in the history of the American military back to school to learn how to shoot.

Dick Bong was just fine with the whole plan, though he did want to get back into combat again as soon as he could. He knew his mother and girlfriend would be perfectly fine with his being grounded, too. The general had honored his request to attend gunnery school. And he figured that teaching assignment when he got back to New Guinea would not be long-lasting. Or maybe some of it could even be accomplished on the job, while shooting down enemy fighters.

The biggest plus in being yanked out of combat? It might rescue him from all those reporters.

Best of all, he could likely spend Mother's Day in May with his family and get quality time with Marge. Maybe he would even pop the question.

One thing still nagged at him, though. Uncaring as he was about any scoreboard or ace race, he still felt he deserved credit for number twenty-eight. Confirmation for that Oscar he had chased all the way down to the water. And then sent somersaulting across the waves with a well-placed shot.

He had no idea how or if he could ever receive the recognition, though. Still, before he packed his duffel bag and set off for the long trip to Washington, DC, and then home, he prevailed upon General Kenney to see what he could do.

The general admitted he had no idea how he might get it done. But at least he owed the kid the effort.

He promised to do what he could.

CHAPTER TWENTY-ONE

CREDIT WHERE CREDIT IS DUE

General George Churchill Kenney was clearly a very busy man, overseeing the efforts of the Army Air Forces in the Southwest Pacific. And even though he and the USAAF were finally turning the course of the air war, trying to keep up with General MacArthur and his almost manic push toward the Philippines made his job even more complicated. Despite how hectic his job was, Kenney felt an obligation to pursue young Dick Bong's request. He had promised the kid that he would do what he could to get him confirmation for the final enemy plane he was so certain he had shot down west of Hollandia on his last mission before heading home on leave.

The general could not imagine why Bong was so adamant about this one claim when he was typically complacent about such things and often willingly gave away credit to fellow pilots for kills that he almost certainly deserved. Maybe the kid thought this one—number twenty-eight—might be his last kill of the war. He was going home for a while, at least four months, and he was aware he would be a gunnery instructor for a bit when he came back. He also knew that the policy at that time was not to send top performers back into combat, no matter how badly their skills were needed.

Before departing for home, Bong laid out for Kenney the details of the combat action he wanted confirmed. The "probable" he sought to convert to "confirmed" had gone down in Tanah-merah Bay, twenty miles west of Hollandia, on April 12. Bong handed the general a photograph of the bay with a big circle drawn around where the enemy Oscar had been hit and then sunk. It included a shadow of a submerged coral reef that the target had struck before beginning to flip. Bong shared in detail how his .50-caliber rounds had ripped into the enemy plane's left wing and had also struck the cockpit and engine, almost certainly hitting the pilot and doing damage to the engine. Then the airplane had gone under so quickly that it had not had the opportunity to catch fire.

"Look, son," Kenney told his newest major. "As you know, with no witness or film, the only way we can officially confirm this is to inspect the wreckage. Right now that area is under enemy control. If that changes, we'll see what we can do."

The general resisted the impulse to ask the kid why this one was so important to him. Bong politely thanked him and left for Wisconsin by way of Washington, DC. He had another meeting scheduled with Hap Arnold there in his new office at the recently occupied Pentagon.

As it happened, US troops had captured Hollandia and fully taken charge of the territory to the west by the time Bong left New Guinea. When General Kenney saw on his desk a dispatch that casually mentioned the Allies were now firmly in control of the area that included Tanahmerah Bay, a light came on. He told one of his aides to relay word that as soon as it was practical, he wanted a diver to go down in the area Bong had circled on the aerial photo. There the diver was to search for the wreckage of a Nakajima Ki-43 and to document details of its condition.

Kenney got the report only a few days later. The diver had had no trouble at all locating the hulk. Partly for inspection, as per General Kenney's request, but also to assure that the wreckage did not drift and become a navigation hazard, a salvage vessel and crew pulled the Oscar to the surface and brought it ashore.

The report: Eleven bullet holes had caused severe damage to the plane's left wing. Though partly decomposed, the pilot's body revealed bullet wounds to his head and neck that had almost certainly been fatal. The Oscar's engine had been damaged by gunfire. There was no sign of significant fire. In other words, the Japanese fighter was located precisely where and in the exact condition Dick Bong had reported.

Kenney proudly submitted the paperwork necessary to grant his top ace credit for number twenty-eight.

While Bong was home dodging reporters and fans as best he could, things were moving rapidly back in New Guinea. As May began, with Hollandia in Allied hands, the Fifth Air Force moved headquarters to the former Japanese base there. That put US forces strategically closer to the Philippines, to which General MacArthur—now finally with the backing of President Roosevelt—wanted to advance. It also meant a move and a promotion for one of the top contenders who could be gaining ground on Dick Bong while he was away.

Tommy McGuire, like Lynch and Bong, had been stuck in one of those staff positions. However, his assignment required far more desk time than theirs had. He had not been allowed nearly as much freedom to fly. Then, early in May, at about the same time as Bong was making his long trip home, McGuire received word that he was about to be back into the war in a big way. He was to be promoted to the rank of major and become commander of the 431st Fighter Squadron. That meant he and the members of his squadron would be regularly flying missions into prime hunting ground, to Japanese air bases located on islands at the far western end of New Guinea.

With plenty of targets to shoot and missions to fly, McGuire assumed he would once again be able to demonstrate his own remarkable abilities to stalk and shoot down enemy airplanes while managing to bring his own P-38 safely back to his new home at Hollandia. He even spent some time flying with aviation hero but still controversial figure Charles Lindbergh.

Between the wars, Lindbergh had been a member of a very vocal isolationist group that lobbied strongly against any involvement again by the United States in a European conflict. His hero status gave him a powerful but divisive anti-war voice. After the Japanese attack on Pearl Harbor and the declaration of war against America by Japan, Germany, and Italy, the US was no longer on the sidelines. Once the war was a reality, Lindbergh was mostly shunned and even dubbed a Nazi sympathizer by some.

However, many in the USAAF saw his expertise in aeronautics as having value in the war effort. Lindbergh came to New Guinea to consult on methods that might be employed to extend the range of American fighters and bombers, including the P-38s. As a consultant for Pan American Airways, he had found ways to greatly improve the fuel usage of the airline's Clipper aircraft, which flew very long overseas routes around the world. Lindbergh's suggestions mostly involved adjustments to the engines and a few changes in how pilots flew their planes. His ideas worked extremely well. That additional range would be invaluable when bombing raids extended farther westward, toward Borneo, Southeast Asia, Malaysia, and the Philippines. McGuire's squadron was soon flying the longest-distance missions of the war up to that point.

But Lindbergh did more than consult. Even though he was civilian, he flew along on combat missions in Lightnings, often with Tommy McGuire, and even fired his own guns on enemy targets while conducting strafing runs. A couple of times, Lindbergh, who would pilot whatever fighter was unoccupied at the time, even took Dick Bong's P-38 up and accompanied squads on missions against the enemy. There is no record of his firing or being fired upon when he was flying *Marge*, though.

While flying another Lightning during an encounter with enemy fighters, Lindbergh was almost shot down. It was his new best friend, Tommy McGuire, who swooped in, chased the Japanese pilot off the hero's tail, and allowed him to return safely back to base.

Meanwhile, McGuire added a few knockdowns to his total, but not nearly enough to make him happy. With so many opportunities, the young pilot from New Jersey by way of Sebring, Florida, was determined to catch and pass Bong's twenty-eight kills while the top gun was away on leave. It was not to be. Mc-Guire came down with a bad case of dengue fever, usually a debilitating and potentially fatal mosquito-borne disease common in the tropics. That had him in and out of hospitals from Hollandia to Port Moresby for much of the Southern Hemisphere winter, radically limiting his possibilities.

By the time Bong returned to New Guinea in early September of 1944, McGuire still had only twenty-one confirmed kills, keeping him in second place among all active AAF pilots, but much further behind Bong than he had wanted or intended to be. But McGuire was still pushing to win the race, promising everybody that he would pull ahead as soon as the docs would allow him to fly all the missions he desired.

For his part, Bong had few comments on a race in which he did not necessarily care to be a participant. He had new knowledge about how to use the guns on their aircraft to best advantage—or at least he felt he did—and he wanted to impart it to his fellow pilots. While General Kenney had given Dick permission to fly combat patrols, he was strictly ordered to fire only in self-defense so long as he was supposed to be a gunnery instructor. Before heading back to the war, he had assured his family and Marge Vattendahl that he might be on his way back into the war zone, but he would be serving only as an instructor, not a combat fighter pilot.

Mostly he was just glad to be farther away from all those reporters, from all the well-intentioned but tiring attention, and from his obligations to answer the same questions and deliver the same speech over and over and over.

For the entire duration of his time back home, he told everyone that he could not wait to once again climb into the cockpit of a Lightning and take the fight to the Japanese, to make a difference. That meant he was doing his part to help end this war but not getting killed doing it.

That, he figured, would be the most direct way to return home, get back to his family, to the farm, and to the woman he intended to marry and spend a long, happy life with.

CHAPTER TWENTY-TWO

PR, PROPOSAL, AND A PROMISE KEPT

Bong had his second audience with General Henry "Hap" Arnold within six months on May 9, 1944, again without first going anywhere close to Poplar, Wisconsin. The fact that the very important and extremely busy senior officer requested the second meeting with the young fighter pilot tells us plenty. It is evidence of not only how valuable the commanding general of the Army Air Forces—the man who was overseeing the air war in both Europe and the Pacific—felt this kid was, but how interested he was to hear thoughts on how the war was going from someone who was so recently amid it all. And, of course, from someone who was such a favorite of General George Kenney.

Arnold also had a long list of things he wanted the top ace to do while he was back in the US. Yes, Bong would get three weeks of leave time, enough to go home and visit. But even during that time, he would be required to make speeches, hold press conferences, and talk with trainees. Then Bong was to go to Matagorda,

Texas, for five weeks to complete the gunnery course for which he had been lobbying.

Though he was constantly being hounded by reporters, his first official news conference would come two days after he had met with Arnold. It would be in the new Pentagon, with Secretary of War Henry Stimson sitting only a few feet away. Bong had spent much of the previous day getting briefed on what to say and how to say it, but the young pilot had already developed a considerable dislike for his military "handlers" as well as for most members of the press. He ended up, much to the dismay of the Army public affairs officer at his side, telling the reporters and a group of USAAF officers exactly how he felt about things rather than sticking to the canned responses. That, of course, made him even more of a target for the members of the media, who were always looking for any new angle for a story that might help them land their articles on the front page.

Such candor at this press event included Bong saying that while American fighter pilots were generally better fliers than their Japanese adversaries, the USAAF boys were not nearly as well trained in some ways. And especially in aerial gunnery. Not at all the prescribed response!

When a reporter asked why General Kenney had taken his best fighter pilot out of service and sent him home, Bong deadpanned, "To keep me from getting killed." Partly true, but still not the answer the Army would have preferred him to give.

Before the PR officer could usher Bong out of the room, another reporter asked him what he intended to do after the war ended. This time his answer bothered no one.

"I want to keep on flying for sure," he answered. "I'll never give it up as long as I am physically fit. I'd like to have a cottage on Lake Gordon [a large natural lake in northern Wisconsin full of muskie, largemouth bass, and walleye] with a big fireplace . . . and a hangar."

In many of his subsequent news conferences during this period back in the US, when he grew tired of answering questions, Bong would stand, point to the public affairs officer who was always hovering at his elbow, and announce, "Well, that's enough from me. I haven't any more. Ask him. He knows it all."

Eddie Rickenbacker was visiting someone at the Pentagon later the same day of the press conference. Eager to shake the hand of the pilot who had broken his record, he made it a point to track down Bong. But when they tried to talk flying, reporters and admirers would not let them alone. They finally left the area and found a spot on the steps of the Pentagon where they could sit in the sunshine and briefly compare notes. They got to chat for only a few moments before Dick was hustled off to meet and greet still more dignitaries and journalists.

The next day, he attended a session of the US Senate, where he was singled out and given a standing ovation by the assemblage. Then he was a guest for lunch with a group of influential senators. Bong was not especially awed by the politicians. He was only thankful he did not have to make a speech.

He was finally released from further obligations on Saturday, May 13, and he promptly hopped on a westbound train. Along the way home, he stopped in Pittsburgh, Pennsylvania, to visit fleetingly with the widow of his friend and fellow pilot Tommy Lynch, who had died while he and Bong were strafing the enemy corvette. Dick shared some anecdotes and presented her with a few snapshots he had of Tommy; then he was back aboard the train and on his way home.

He arrived at the station in Chicago early on Mother's Day. There to greet him was not only his mom, Dora, but also his father and—surprise!—Marge. There was a grand reunion right there on the platform.

The plan was to drive cross-state all the way home, but there was one more obligation first. Not for Dick this time. For Dora. She was to meet up with the mothers of two other USAAF aces and then the three women were to be part of a special Mother's Day broadcast from the studios of the powerful radio station WLS. Only then could they begin the long drive to Poplar, which did, at least, offer them plenty of time to catch up.

It took Dick two more weeks after getting home before he finally got around to proposing to Marge. They were on a drive, in the middle of farm country, when he abruptly pulled over into a field alongside the narrow road. He opened the car's glove box, pulled out a ring, placed it on her finger, and shyly asked her to be his wife. She later reported that she happily said, "Yes!" without hesitation.

They spread the word about the engagement, and reporters promptly picked up on that bit of positive personal news, too. America's top fighter ace getting engaged to his sweetheart back home was big news. However, the couple assured everyone that they had not yet set a date for the wedding. That would come only when any possibility of Dick being in combat had ended. And for now nobody knew when that would be.

Part of why it took so long after his arrival for Dick to propose was the fault of the Army Air Forces. But some of it was his own responsibility, too. The Army had several appearances in the area scheduled for him and they were not optional events. There always seemed to be this reporter or that one who wanted a personal interview or to take snapshots of the all-American hero on leave in his idyllic hometown.

But Dick had some things he wanted to do, too. And he intended for that special moment with Marge to be just right.

For one, his brother Carl "Bud" Bong Jr. was set to graduate from Poplar High School on June 3. Dick happily agreed not only to attend the commencement ceremony but to stand onstage and hand a diploma to each grad, including Carl, who would later pen two books about his famous sibling.

But the one thing Dick most wanted to do while he was home—besides be with Marge—took considerable amounts of both time and effort. Somehow, he tracked down an airworthy P-38 Lightning at a nearby Army Air Forces facility. We do not know how he managed it, but he talked whoever was responsible for the plane into allowing him to gas it up on several occasions and fly it all around the northern part of Wisconsin. Fly it with spectacular results.

He happily buzzed Poplar, including the homes of his parents and other relatives. He gave Marge's family, his future in-laws, the same extemporaneous air show. He also did aerobatics over local war-matériel factories and training bases, all to the delight of those dedicated workers. The *Evening Telegram* in Superior ran a picture of a P-38 doing a very low and very fast flyover of the Walter Butler Shipyard facility there.

So far as we know, nobody complained. No laundry was blown off a clothesline. Nor was there any panic, as would typically have been the case if a strange plane showed up and buzzed towns during wartime. Indeed, everybody—including the Superior newspaper—somehow knew it was only their own star, top-scoring ace pilot Dick Bong, who was up there putting on a free show for the local folk.

Inevitably, his time at home had to come to an end. There was another quick trip back to Washington on his itinerary. That was to prepare him for the long trek cross-country he was about to undertake, traveling from Florida to California to make frequent war bond speeches to cheering crowds along the way.

He did receive one bit of heartening information, and ironically, the good news came from a reporter. He informed Bong that he had been granted official credit for that last Oscar, the one he had knocked out of the sky and into the bay west of Hollandia. General Kenney had kept his promise to look for the wreckage in the water and try to get him credit.

Number twenty-eight was no longer a "probable." It was confirmed.

"I was sure I got him," Bong told the reporter. "I . . . chased him out over the water. I kept pouring lead at him and I guess he must have run into some of my bullets because he crashed into the bay."

Bong wrapped up the last leg of his PR tour in July and headed down to Texas to once again become a student. He had no idea what the future held for him. Truth was, he was a much better shooter than he admitted. Fellow pilots had kidded him about his claims of requiring more training in the fine art of aiming and firing at enemy aircraft. He just wanted a taxpayer-funded trip home to see that pretty gal of his. After all, those men had seen firsthand evidence of Dick's abilities in that department. And his twenty-eight kills provided even more proof.

As General Kenney would later write, there were a couple of reasons why he, who mostly agreed with Bong's peers, had gone along with the idea of the airman going back to gunnery school. First, it would keep Bong out of danger for another five weeks. And second, the kid would not necessarily become any more skilled as a shooter, but he would be a better teacher after he came back.

Marge wrote in her memoirs that she doubted her husband-to-be would remain an instructor for very long once he was back in the Pacific Theater of Operations. She knew how desperately he wanted to return to combat. How he was convinced he could help hasten the end of the conflict, but only if he was flying missions against the enemy.

Dick, too, told some of his contemporaries that he did not expect to stay out of the war for very long. He intended to saddle up and go shoot Oscars and Zeros no later than the end of September. Indeed, by the time he returned to New Guinea, to General Kenney's new headquarters at Hollandia, on September 10, 1944, Dick Bong was already scheming how he would get back into combat.

CHAPTER TWENTY-THREE

THE SHARPSHOOTING INSTRUCTOR

I know you'll knock down another twenty or thirty Nips,"
General George Kenney told Dick Bong. "But if, instead,
you can teach a hundred pilots to get one Jap apiece without getting themselves shot down, I'll be way ahead of the game."

Kenney's logic made perfect sense to the returning ace, but
he did not necessarily like it. Finally, the general agreed that if
he would teach for a month, he would then give Dick permission to occasionally go out on missions, primarily so he could
observe directly how his lessons might be benefiting the other
pilots. No attacking allowed, mind you. Just shooting in self-
defense. If necessary. Meanwhile, Bong needed to learn Lindbergh's methods for extending flying range, or the gang would
simply fly away from him when he had to turn his thirsty Lightning back for gas.

As Bong was pressuring the boss for combat time, so was his

top challenger, Tommy McGuire. Number two in confirmed kills but still eight behind Bong, McGuire had come down with a nasty case of malaria just as he was recovering from dengue fever. That had quashed any chances he had for catching Dick during his time back in the States. When McGuire left the hospital and was feeling better—he was down to less than 120 pounds—he sought an audience with Kenney to argue his case.

The general mollified his most competitive pilot a bit by agreeing to put him back in the cockpit of a P-38, but only after getting clearance to do so from the Army docs. He also reminded McGuire that Bong would be a professor for a while yet and, for the most part, out of combat for the next month. There was also the fact that enemy fighters would likely be few and far between for the near future. And except for some missions against some key enemy petroleum facilities in Borneo, that would probably remain the case, at least until the coming massive assault to retake the Philippine Islands.

Other than some plinking and plunking, that turned out to true. Bombing raids against the widely scattered enemy outposts in the westernmost islands of New Guinea were successful but scared up few enemy fighters in response. Where the Japanese once controlled the Pacific from Malaysia to the Solomons and from Borneo to the Philippines, they had now pulled back to take another stand, to protect their occupation of the Philippines, and to hopefully maintain the territory from which they got so many vital natural resources for the war effort.

Meanwhile, McGuire partially recovered from his tropical ailments while Bong, based in Nadzab, traveled from airfield to airfield in the region, demonstrating how to shoot down planes without having to fly so close and head-on.

It was October 10, exactly one month after Dick had reported back and had his chat with General Kenney, that he chose to ride along on a major attack mission on its way to hit a big Japanese oil refinery on the eastern coast of the island of Borneo. It was a target well out of reach of P-38 escorts before Lindbergh's tweaks and the capture and occupation of the advance base at Hollandia.

Before committing to allow Dick to fly with the attackers, Kenney once again made sure his ace understood the conditions under which he was to join combat flights. That he was only to observe, to shoot if shot at. There were thirty-five other Lightnings in the formation, protecting more than a hundred bombers. Dick was to sit back, watch, and see how the new gunnery techniques he had brought back with him were being applied.

By the end of the day, the Empire of Japan had lost five dozen fighters and their pilots. (Almost always, if an Imperial Japanese Army Air Service plane went down, the pilot was killed. Most Japanese pilots carried no parachutes. To bail out was tantamount to surrender, something they had sworn not to do. Going down with the plane was a form of ritualistic suicide.)

Of the sixty enemy planes shot down that day, gunnery instructor and observer Dick Bong was responsible for two.

Back at Hollandia safely, Bong was honest but typically terse and straightforward in his incident report. When Kenney reviewed the action, two numbers jumped out at him. One of Bong's fatal shots had come at 1,500 feet. The other action occurred at better than three miles high. Didn't sound all that self-defensive to the general!

When confronted, Dick said he was doing just as he had been told to do. Observing. But then he had spotted a Nakajima JIN Gekko fighter-reconnaissance plane way down near the deck. It appeared to be hurrying back toward Borneo. Bong told Kenney he figured the guy was rushing back to warn the Japanese of the size of the approaching Allied force so they could send even more fighters to stop the assault. So Bong had dived on him, caught him by surprise, and put him into the sea. Practically no risk involved. The enemy pilot never saw Bong coming.

The second one? Definitely self-defense, Bong claimed. When he had climbed back up to where the fighting was, one of the Zeros had taken a run at several of Dick's teammates and then at him. He had had no choice. He put the guy down.

"From long range, I assume," Kenney shot back. That was the reason for all the training Bong had taken and was now teaching, after all. To be able to shoot targets from greater distances and at sharp angles off the nose.

"Well, the first one was too easy," Bong responded. "I was right on top of him. No choice on the second one. I put my gun barrel in his cockpit and got him with one burst 'cause he was on top of me."

Kenney could only shake his head. And give the kid another firm reminder that he was to take no chances out there.

All signs were, though, that Kenney's pilots were shooting just fine. While taking down those sixty enemy fighters, the

AAF had lost only one P-38 and four bombers. Bong's report about how his instruction had helped the aim of the other pilots was encouraging. The improved shooting percentage was obvious. "If I had had this kind of training at the start," Bong told Kenney, referring to what he had learned at Matagorda, "I would have seventy-five confirmed now instead of thirty."

Kenney could not wait to tell his boss about the kid's success and his new kill score of thirty. Even if he had clearly stretched the definition of "self-defense" by a bit. The general wired the news to Hap Arnold that night. Kenney made certain to convey that he had forcefully reiterated his instructions to Bong not to take such chances in the future, but to shoot only if shot at.

"Congratulations to Major Bong on his continued mastery of the manly art of self-defense," Arnold shot back. "Feel sure your warning will have desired effect."

Even from 9,000 miles away, it was clear Arnold's tongue remained firmly in his cheek.

Both Bong and McGuire—once the doctors approved his return to the tussle—received new-model Lightnings, the recently arrived P-38L-1. Its most obvious feature was its increased power and improved handling at top speed, but it had also been modified to take advantage of Charles Lindbergh's engine tweaks. McGuire promptly put his wife's nickname on his fifth P-38, making it *Pudgy V*. But Dick Bong postponed putting Marge's picture or name or any of the flag emblems on his new bird. He told everyone he was not really supposed to be in combat, and with all the instructing he was doing, he had not yet had time to take care of the task. The truth was, after the *Stars and*

Stripes story with the photo of his plane and all the bothersome attention it had caused Marge, he simply did not want to put her through all that hassle again. Especially if something happened to him.

He explained his decision to her in a letter home. She understood and appreciated it. And her thoughts on the subject were the only ones that mattered to him.

Of course, that did not really keep the attention off the pretty young college girl with the hero boyfriend-fiancé. When word got out that Bong had added two more kills to his total, that he had left colorful Fast Eddie Rickenbacker in the dust, the press ran with it. That was the roundabout way Marge Vattendahl found out that her "instructor"—despite his assurances to her and Dora Bong—was still actively sparring with enemy fighter planes.

In an exchange of letters, Marge gave him what for for giving her the impression that he was no more than a teacher. He countered, assuring her he had been grounded again and was as safe as anybody could be in that part of the world. It was not a lie. General Kenney had forbidden him from inserting himself into any more strikes against the huge refinery—or what was left of it—in Borneo, and that was about all the action to be had in early October of 1944.

Tommy McGuire was not supposed to be part of the future attacks on the crucial enemy petroleum facility, either. That was because his unit had not been assigned any missions to that lone hot spot. But he was so anxious to get ahead of Dick Bong that he simply went AWOL, did not bother to tell his squadron commander, and joined the 9th Fighter Squadron for a run there on October 14. He was but one P-38 of a total of sixty that were to escort more than a hundred B-24 bombers. The party crasher proceeded to knock down four enemy planes that day. One kill had no witnesses, so he was officially credited with three. McGuire now had twenty-four confirmed, still trailing Bong by six.

McGuire received a dressing-down from his commander for simply abandoning his group and flying off to fight with another. Even though he had had no assignment that day. But again, as with Bong, it was difficult to be too hard on a guy who had shot down four Japanese airplanes. And by then, things had gotten a bit loosey-goosey with all the freelancing the top pilots were being allowed to do. There was never any formal reprimand for McGuire for ignoring Air Forces combat assignment protocol.

McGuire and the others had done such a good job that day—and in previous runs, including the one with Bong riding along—that what had once been a major refinery was pretty much out of business by mid-October. No need to go there anymore. In fact, the big island of Borneo was declared a nonfactor and would be bypassed by US forces for the rest of the war. (Australian troops liberated the island in July 1945, then continued mop-up operations through the end of the war.) But that meant the two dueling aces once again had very little at which to shoot.

However, that was about to change. Out to the northwest, all holy hell would soon be unleashed by the Allies. By far the biggest assault of the war in the Pacific to that point was coming. General Douglas MacArthur was about to, by God, keep a sacred promise. And that inferno would offer a perfect chance for Tommy McGuire and Richard Bong to shoot down as many enemy aircraft as they could manage.

One of them would excel and set a record likely never to be broken.

The other would fail tragically in his quest to become America's top gun.

CHAPTER TWENTY-FOUR

HAPPY SKEPTICISM

The first Allied troops who were a part of the immense assault to begin the liberation of the Philippines went ashore on the island of Leyte on October 20, 1944. It was preceded by a two-day naval battle in the Leyte Gulf in which some miscalculations by the Japanese, some savvy moves by the ships of Admiral William "Bull" Halsey's Third Fleet and Admiral Thomas Kinkaid's Seventh Fleet, and some plain old good luck led to the virtual annihilation of what remained of the empire's once-proud naval fleet. Historians generally agree that the Battle of Leyte Gulf was the largest naval battle in history—and that it was a significant victory for the US and its allies.

That meant the Japanese, now mostly without carriers and carrier-based aircraft, would have to rely on ground troops and airpower from land bases if they had any hopes of hanging on to the island chain. There was no doubt in anybody's mind that they would fight to the last soldier and pilot to do so.

The island of Leyte was taken surprisingly easily. It was here that the iconic picture of Douglas MacArthur wading ashore—fulfilling his promise to return to the Philippines—was taken. That location today is MacArthur Leyte Landing National Park and features a larger-than-life statue that re-creates that moment.

In many cases, there were signs the enemy had fled their bases at the last minute, leaving only snipers, mines, and booby traps to slow the progress of the US Army. There were practically no air attacks against ground troops as they moved in, though aircraft did continue to strafe Allied shipping in the gulf as well as engineers and construction workers trying to repair for use troop barracks and aircraft landing fields. Though the strikes by enemy planes were primarily harassing, men did still die, and progress was delayed.

One prime objective early in the ground invasion by the Allies was the capture of the town of Tacloban, located at the head of Leyte Gulf. That was because it was the home of a very good airfield. Good, that is, before planes off US Navy carriers had obliterated much of it as part of the assault. The town would also become the location of General MacArthur's headquarters until he could return to Manila and reclaim his old digs, which were still occupied by the Japanese commander overseeing the empire's forces in the Philippines.

General Kenney was among the first of the high-ranking officers to arrive in Tacloban after it had been secured. He wanted to personally supervise the restoration of bombed-out buildings around the airfield and the repair of the shell-pocked runway there as well as one at a nearby aerodrome in the town of Dulag. He knew it would be crucial to start moving in aircraft quickly and to begin bombing runs to support the long, hard slog to Manila.

The first Army P-38s—three dozen of them—landed in Tacloban on October 27, just as American aircraft carriers were leaving the area to refuel, refit, rearm, and repair battle damage as well as replace planes and pilots lost in the massive sea battle. The workers had had time only to fill in most of the bomb craters and to put down 3,000 feet of steel mat for the runway. That made it a marginally short landing and takeoff strip for Lightnings. Kenney had sent word that he had room and support personnel for about thirty-four P-38s, and they would need to be flown in by the best pilots, fliers comfortable landing and taking off on a short runway.

Kenney was lunching with General MacArthur at Tacloban when the roar of the engines signaled the approach of the '38s arriving in perfect, low, and loud formation, announcing to everyone on the ground that the Army Air Forces intended to dominate the skies over the Philippines. Both generals abandoned their meal, jumped into MacArthur's staff car, and rushed out to happily greet the Lightnings as they landed. MacArthur and Kenney made it a point to shake hands with each pilot after he had taxied off the end of the short runway and exited his airplane. MacArthur knew most of them by their names and reputations if not by their faces. After all, the men in that group were Kenney's top fighter pilots, responsible for downing more than 500 enemy warplanes in the war so far. He thrilled them all by telling them with obvious sincerity, "You don't know how glad I am to see you!"

Then Kenney spotted his cherub and gunnery instructor,

Dick Bong, off to the side, already out of his cockpit and checking over his unnamed airplane after the long flight in. The general motioned for him to come over.

"Bong, who the hell told you to come up here?" Kenney later recalled asking the kid.

With a shy grin and a glance in the direction of General MacArthur, Bong replied, "General Whitehead gave me permission."

"Did he tell you that you had permission to fly combat?"

"No, but can I?"

That reply resulted in a good laugh from everyone. There is still speculation about whether or not Kenney knew that his top ace would be among the first to arrive in the Philippines. Some say that conversation was for the benefit of General MacArthur and, eventually, for Hap Arnold, whose staff back in Washington preferred such prime PR heroes as Richard Bong not be placed in harm's way. Regardless, Kenney's answer to the kid's question was quick and to the point.

"I'd say anybody who can crank a P-38 and get it off the ground is welcome to fly combat missions in these parts right about now."

Later that same day, about five p.m., the field's newly installed radar system picked up an approaching flight of five enemy aircraft, maybe ten minutes away. The radar was still not calibrated but there was no doubt that enemy fighters were en route, bound to pester men on bulldozers and others scrambling in the rafters, repairing hangars, just as they had been doing most of the week. This time, though, the attackers would encounter a rather substantial greeting party.

Four P-38s were in the air by the time the Japanese planes showed up. One of them was being flown by Richard Ira Bong. The US pilots quickly shot down four of the five enemy aircraft. The lone survivor hightailed it back to his base, certainly ready to share the bad news that the dreaded "one pilot, two airplanes" had come over from New Guinea and they were now in the skies above the Philippines.

Bong was credited with one of the kills, an Oscar. He went after another Oscar, was sure he damaged him, but lost him in the clouds. Not even five hours at the battlefront and he had already made his mark. And all this even though he was still not officially authorized to be taking part in combat.

It would not be long, though, before Dick Bong did more damage, spectacularly and in full view of the general and most of the personnel at Tacloban. That action would lead to a droll exchange of messages between George Kenney, now in the newly created role of the commanding general of the Fifth Air Force on MacArthur's staff, and General Henry "Hap" Arnold. Those messages between two of World War II's highest-ranking and most powerful men would be tacked up on a bulletin board at the new staff headquarters in Tacloban for all to see and enjoy.

It was the very next day after his arrival. Dick was asked by the Tacloban commanding officer to go up and scout around for a location reasonably close by where they might build an alternative landing strip. The one at Dulag was proving to be difficult to reclaim from the mud, and even with its runway soon to be extended, Tacloban would not have nearly the capacity necessary to handle all the bombers and other aircraft that would soon need runways on Leyte. Bong had not been in the air for a minute before he was informed that—ready or not—radar had indicated a couple of enemy fighters were angrily zooming his way.

He did not hesitate or consider whether or not he was authorized to engage. He flew to where the radar operator told him the incoming planes would be, intercepted them, and promptly took care of both of them. The entire showdown took a little over a minute. No doubt about whether or not Bong would receive credit, either. The entire scuffle was well within sight of the base and just about everybody saw him shoot down two enemy fighters and send their pilots to the afterlife to meet their ancestors.

That night, George Kenney sent a dispatch to Hap Arnold, saying, "In accordance with my instructions, Major Richard Bong is trying to be careful, but the Nips won't do their part. On the twenty-seventh, five hours after arriving at Tacloban, Bong was again forced to defend himself and number thirty-one resulted. On the twenty-eighth, while looking for suitable locations for aerodromes in the vicinity of Tacloban, he was assaulted by two more Nips who became numbers thirty-two and thirty-three. Unless he was bothered again today, this is his latest score."

Arnold's response came two days later. "Major Bong's excuses in matter of shooting down three more Nips noted with happy skepticism by this headquarters. In Judge Advocate's opinion, he is liable under Articles of War 122 (willful or negligent damage to enemy equipment or personnel)."

While the Articles of War is an actual list of dos and don'ts for combatants during wartime, there are only 121 of them. Arnold made up number 122. And everyone who saw the messages on the base bulletin board had a good laugh about the conversation between the two generals.

On October 27, Tommy McGuire was piloting one in a collection of twenty P-38s headed to Tacloban, the second group of Lightnings summoned by Kenney the instant he felt the field was ready to accommodate them. Before the airmen arrived, though, they encountered a swarm of ten Japanese fighters along the way. The Lightnings promptly engaged and eliminated six of them.

McGuire got one, increasing his score to twenty-three.

When he landed, his first question was "So how many does Bong have now?"

We can only surmise he was mightily disappointed by the answer.

CHAPTER TWENTY-FIVE

THE SOCIETY OF THE BRAVEST
OF THE BRAVE

With the USAAF's top two fighter pilots now flying out of the same air base in the Philippines, and even living for a while in the same quarters, the competition promptly heated up dramatically. Even if it was mostly one-way between the fliers themselves. Though Dick Bong continued to hold his lead, with the sudden abundance of enemy targets, Tommy McGuire was now matching him kill for kill, keeping pace but not gaining on him.

Bong gets two. McGuire gets two. Bong adds one. McGuire bags one. But Dick always managed to hold an eight-kill lead. That was a mounting source of exasperation for McGuire.

Though others in the two squadrons now operating out of Tacloban and Dulag in the Philippines were taking down their share of enemy fighters, it was all they could do to keep pace with the pair of leaders and their amazing success. They were not gaining on Bong and McGuire at all. No one else in the Army

Air Forces in either the Pacific or Europe was close, either. For a variety of reasons—the number of enemy targets, far less airspace to cover—many more Allied pilots in Europe qualified as aces than did those in the Pacific, but even the top ones among them had between fifteen and twenty kills against the Luftwaffe. It was becoming more and more difficult to add significantly to their totals. With D-day forces advancing from the west and with the debacle in Russia, Hitler was able to put fewer and fewer aircraft in the sky to blunt Allied bombers and their escorts.

Back in the Pacific, carrier-based Navy pilot Commander David McCampbell was effectively matching the two Army fliers, though. And he was getting his targets in big gulps, including shooting down nine enemy fighters over the Philippine Sea in a single day, on October 24. By the end of the first week of November, McCampbell was within two kills of matching Dick Bong. Flying off the carrier USS *Essex* (CV-9), the Alabamian would end the war with thirty-four aerial victories, tops in the Navy but not quite catching Bong. McCampbell did receive the Medal of Honor. His record of nine kills in a single day still stands.

Meanwhile, much of the rest of the planet was watching with rapt attention the competition between Bong and McGuire, almost as if their favorite baseball teams were locked in a tight pennant struggle. Indeed, *Stars and Stripes* helped military personnel stay apprised of the competition with a weekly update that looked very similar to a major-league standings update.

As for Bong and McGuire now operating from the same location, there is no evidence of friction between them. Each considered the other a friend. Or at least as much a friend as pilots in the war allowed themselves to be, considering the odds of their coming back from their missions alive. Even though the press tried to pit them as bitter rivals in and out of the cockpit, no one who was there at the time saw any animosity between the two aces. Several reporters tried to get McGuire—usually depicted as the aggressive one, with the black mustache and Hollywood good looks—to say something headline worthy about Bong—who was always portrayed as being quiet, modest, reserved—but he gave them only "We're friends. We are not going to be involved in a competition that might put our lives at risk. We're here to win the war."

McGuire suffered a couple of minor injuries—one in the derriere and the other in the head—in separate midair incidents in November. However, although he missed little air time and continued to keep pace with Bong, he still could not manage to catch him. He seemed in lockstep at eight behind. By then, Dick had thirty-six and Bong had tallied twenty-eight.

When McGuire hit twenty-six—the Rickenbacker number—the media had made much of the milestone, primarily to keep the rivalry hot. That had given McGuire's wife, Marilynn, who was waiting for him back in San Antonio, some renewed hope that her hero husband would soon be sent home for his own spectacular war bond tour. Like Richard Bong's. It was by then approaching two years since she and Tommy had seen each other. In letters to her husband, she had made much of the facts that

Bong had been back to the States twice in that time; that he had met and proposed to a girl; that he had been in the company of high-ranking military and political figures and paraded before the media and entertainers as the symbol of the American war effort. All this while Tommy was out there suffering from dengue fever and malaria and continuing to do his job. Surely it was time for him to get some Stateside leave. Like Richard Bong. McGuire wrote back that though previous promises of time off had fallen through, he was now hearing that he would be sent home in time to be with her for Christmas. Certainly, no later than New Year's.

It did not happen.

December 7, 1944, was not only the well-noted third anniversary of the attack on Pearl Harbor but also a big day of action in the Philippines, which had been hit by the Japanese ten hours after the Pearl Harbor assault (December 8 on that side of the International Date Line). Despite their lackluster defense of Leyte upon MacArthur's initial invasion in October, the Japanese had merely sagged back then to create a much stiffer line. That included not only continually importing reinforcement troops to replace those the Allies were taking out but also employing a new tactic: the kamikaze aircraft attack. The latter was causing considerable damage to the American shipping so necessary to restock and rearm the immense numbers of invading troops. Two destroyers escorting troopships were lost to the suicide planes on December 7.

The big victory that day came among the clouds. Before the day was over, the USAAF had taken down almost sixty Japanese fighters—some of which were likely kamikazes—and a number of bombers. Only three of the Army planes were lost but their pilots were rescued.

Dick Bong and Tommy McGuire continued their match game. Bong claimed a fighter and a bomber. McGuire got two fighters.

Bong's total was now thirty-eight. McGuire's was thirty. A difference still of eight.

General Kenney was somewhat miffed. He had just submitted paperwork—with the encouragement of General MacArthur, who had told Kenney that such an honor was overdue—to have Dick Bong awarded the Medal of Honor. Rather than for a specific event, it was for all he had done since arriving in the Philippines on October 27. But for the citation, Kenney had listed Bong's total number of enemy aircraft destroyed at thirty-six. Now the kid had gone out and shot down two more—ten planes instead of the eight for which he was being rewarded—and it was too late to add the latest ones to the paperwork.

"Dick already had every other American decoration for valor, and I had given him nothing since he had returned to the theater," Kenney later wrote. "Now I figured that eight Jap aircraft destroyed in a little more than a month, especially when Bong was only supposed to shoot 'in self-defense,' warranted some special recognition."

MacArthur's current policy was to present such high awards privately, within the confines of his headquarters at Tacloban. "I'm not running for public office and don't need the publicity," he maintained. But Kenney prevailed upon the general to do a much larger event in one of the reconstructed USAAF hangars at the airstrip. And there were to be as many of his pilots, support crew members, construction personnel, and even Filipino civilian workers present as possible. It would be a salute to them also, as well as to one of their favorites.

MacArthur reluctantly agreed. He liked the kid, too. And knew he deserved the attention. It would be a morale builder as well.

Before the presentation ceremony, General Kenney was already angling to send his ace out of harm's way as soon as possible. The Medal of Honor would give him the perfect excuse since, as previously noted, it had become common practice to remove living recipients of the medal from the hazards of combat. Plus, those live heroes now had even more value for recruiting, making morale speeches, and leading war bond rallies.

Even so, the general dreaded the inevitable conversation with the kid. Bong had told him repeatedly that he did not want to leave the war until he had collected fifty enemy planes. But the tragic losses of Kearby and Lynch were fresh in everyone's mind.

There were still no firm plans to send Tommy McGuire home, either, even though he continued to write Marilynn that he was hearing he would be there for Christmas. Then by New Year's. Or maybe by mid-January 1945 at the latest.

Kenney finally told Dick Bong that when he got number forty, he was going back to Wisconsin "to marry that girl and be a live hero." Just before Thanksgiving, Dick wrote Marge and his family, saying, "Maybe if I shoot down forty Nips, I'll be sent home to stay. I hope so anyway. I'm just as anxious to get home as you are to have me home."

Then, four days after that letter went into the mail, and while Dick was off duty, there was an incident that brought it all to a head. Midmorning, there was a warning of yet another impending air raid on the base. Pilots on alert scrambled. One ran to the nearest P-38, which was fueled, loaded with ammunition, and parked at the edge of the runway, ready for just such an event.

It was Dick Bong's plane.

Captain John Davis was the man who quickly cranked the engine and took off with his fellow pilots to intercept the incoming enemy fighters. But shortly after takeoff, and minutes before taking on the Japanese, one of the engines on Bong's Lightning virtually exploded. The plane, in a climb and under full power, veered wildly, flipped halfway over on its back, and then went almost straight down into the muddy ground beyond the end of the runway. Davis died instantly.

Any other day, Dick Bong would have been in the cockpit when that engine blew apart while the plane was still straining to gain altitude on takeoff. Good as he was, Dick likely would have had no more luck controlling the plummeting aircraft than Davis had had. And America's top ace would have been lost, not in battle but while taking off in an aircraft, something he did practically every day.

Initial reports had Bong behind the controls. That rumor was quickly quashed. The Army made sure their top ace was visible, alive and well.

With no other P-38 available for him at Tacloban, Bong moved over to Dulag, about thirty miles away. The engineers had finally won the battle against swampy mud and creeping vegetation, and made the runway there usable. In fact, Bong had transferred himself there in the hopes of getting a ride sooner, collecting two more shoot-downs, and seeing if General Kenney was serious about sending him to safety. It had nothing to do with Tommy McGuire, his closest rival, now operating out of Dulag as well. Regardless, the near loss of Bong and now the physical proximity of the two top competing pilots energized their duel for the press.

A ceremony on December 12 did even more to whet the appetites of the reporters. That day, General Douglas MacArthur himself came down to the hangar at the airfield at Tacloban to present Major Richard Ira Bong with his nation's highest award for valor. And George Kenney, the head of the Army Air Forces in the Pacific, was the master of ceremonies. Since Bong had always been one of the general's favorites, Kenney pulled out all the stops. He had eight Lightnings lined up in a semicircle inside the hangar—there was light rain that day—with their crews standing before them. Behind Dick Bong stood his "guard of honor," a dozen P-38 pilots, each of whom had credit for at least a dozen kills. Kenney later estimated there were close to two thousand people gathered there to witness the event.

"Bong stood in front of them, speechless with stage fright, shaking like a leaf," Kenney would write. "In a sky full of Jap airplanes, all shooting in his direction, Dick would be as cool as a cucumber, but there in front of everybody, with the great MacArthur ready to decorate him with the highest award his country could give him, Bong was terrified."

As was typical, MacArthur snapped off a salute to the medal recipient before the kid had a chance to salute the general. But then he did something that was not typically part of such ceremonies. The general's PR staff had written a speech for him to deliver that day, one already provided to the press. However, he kept it in his pocket and ad-libbed something much shorter, totally different, and undoubtedly more heartfelt.

MacArthur stepped toward Bong, put his hands on the young pilot's shoulders, looked him in the eyes, and delivered a one-sentence speech. He was likely speaking as one Medal of Honor recipient to another when he said, "Major Richard Ira Bong, who has ruled the air from New Guinea to the Philippines, I now induct you into the society of the bravest of the brave, the wearers of the Congressional Medal of Honor of the United States."

The citation reads: "For conspicuous gallantry and intrepidity in action above and beyond the call of duty in the Southwest Pacific area from 10 October to 15 November 1944. Though assigned to duty as gunnery instructor and neither required nor expected to perform combat duty, Maj. Bong voluntarily and at his own urgent request engaged in repeated combat missions, including unusually hazardous sorties over Balikpapan, Borneo, and in the Leyte area of the Philippines. His aggressiveness and daring resulted in his shooting down eight enemy airplanes during this period."

After the brief event, Bong slipped away, looking for lunch. He later admitted that he had been so nervous about the award ceremony that he had skipped breakfast. And he had already taken the medal off his chest where MacArthur had pinned it and put it into his uniform shirt pocket. He did not want to appear to be trying to impress anybody.

The day after the ceremony, Tommy McGuire picked up another score—a Mitsubishi J2M, named a "Jack" by the Allies—in action over the island of Cebu. Dick Bong, as per usual, extended his lead back out to eight kills two days later, as he ranged ever farther away from Leyte, over the island of Negros. Both he and Tommy McGuire were part of the same flight originating out of Dulag. Bong took down an Oscar but was not particularly happy about his performance. He twice raced right past the target, doing little damage the first time, but inflicting enough on the second pass to send the Ki-43—or at least large pieces of it—into the Sulu Sea. With nothing else to shoot at, they were home by lunchtime.

McGuire got none on that run. Bong was now at thirty-nine.

Two days later, McGuire and Bong were once again paired with two other fliers as their wingmen as they went looking for targets over Mindoro. Another of the nation's larger islands, Mindoro was not that far south of Manila. US Army troops had come ashore on the island near the town of San Jose and quickly secured the area. Since then, by conducting almost constant bombing and strafing runs, the Japanese had been trying to keep the Allied forces from digging in and constructing a landing strip there. McGuire figured the four pilots could scare up some action in the area and help hasten the opening of a new landing field they could use, so off they went.

But things were slow that morning, and they saw nothing. Considering the distance back to Leyte and Dulag, they were marginally low on fuel. McGuire was just about to make the call to head on back home when two enemy fighters suddenly appeared out of a cloud deck below them. Low on fuel or not, McGuire and Bong pounced on the two unsuspecting foes. With minimal use of ammo and very little wasted gas, both targets quickly became kills.

McGuire now had his thirty-second. Bong had hit forty.

There was no mention of the milestone in Bong's after-incident report, which came at the completion of his 146th wartime combat mission and after almost 400 hours of seat time. Few pilots were asked to complete more than twenty-five missions before being rotated out of a combat role. This day, though, Bong included only his usual spare details in his recap: "The Oscar disintegrated and caught fire and dived straight down and crashed about twenty miles north of San Jose."

Somebody else was well aware of the count. Upon hearing the news, George Kenney sent word that Bong was to leave his P-38 at Dulag and hitch a ride up to Tacloban as soon as possible for a personal meeting. He did not want to risk the kid getting into a brawl during that short hop.

Bong well knew the purpose of the one-on-one get-together with the general. Kenney would later write about their conversation: "I told him that his career as a fighter pilot was now over. General Arnold had continued sending me messages that I should take Bong out of combat. General MacArthur obviously had great affection for the kid and said he would hate to see him listed among those shot down. The whole Forty-ninth Fighter Group—in fact, the whole Fifth Air Force—wanted me to send him home. I, too, was worried about sending the pitcher to the well once too often."

Kenney had decided he would not give Bong the opportunity to try to talk him out of sending the pilot home, no matter how much he might push to be allowed to stick around to get ten more kills. The general was cocked and loaded for an argument when Dick walked into his office.

"He was going home. Forty was a record that would almost certainly stand from then on. I wanted him to go home, marry his girl, and start raising a lot of towheaded Swedes like himself."

Surprisingly to Kenney, America's top fighting ace did not put up any defense at all. He agreed to go Stateside without an argument. It was done. He was to depart the Southwest Pacific two days after Christmas 1944.

Meanwhile, Tommy McGuire finally had the opportunity to make some headway against Dick Bong's forty, the record that General Kenney was so certain would stand forever. McGuire now felt he could push right past that number and well beyond. And so far, there was little talk of sending him home for rest.

While ground troops continued to slog northward, slowly pushing enemy troops back in some of the toughest, bloodiest action of the war, the USAAF drove even more aggressively. By the last week of December, they were staging regular bombing runs against targets on the main Philippine island of Luzon. That included Clark Field, a major prewar air base particularly well used by the Japanese once the Philippines fell into their hands. The Allies were also now targeting key enemy installations in and around Manila, preparing for the eventual ground assault on the nation's capital. Between the massive bomb runs and the Army's eventual artillery barrage, the historic city would mostly be destroyed.

Meanwhile, McGuire's squadron had been moved to new facilities near San Jose on Mindoro. They would now be regular participants in all that action. And that was perfectly fine with the Army's leading active fighter ace.

On Christmas Day, McGuire's group was part of an attack that encountered seventy enemy fighters. They engaged and claimed thirty-nine of them. Five P-38s were shot down but three pilots were rescued. McGuire received credit for three of that day's kills. Thirty-five total. No longer eight behind Bong, now that the general's fair-haired boy would not be adding any more to his record.

The very next day, McGuire again led his squadron on a bomber escort mission toward Clark Field. This time a mere twenty Nippon fighters challenged them. Thirteen of them were knocked down. McGuire got three of those, too.

Thirty-eight. A total of seven kills in about a week. Bong's "unbreakable" record suddenly appeared to be as reachable as Eddie Rickenbacker's had turned out to be.

McGuire's sudden success had General Kenney worried, though. He called McGuire to a hasty meeting in his office.

"You look tired to me, son," Kenney told him. "I'm taking you off flying for a little while so you can get some rest."

Kenney was not exaggerating. The recent illnesses and the pressure McGuire was putting on himself to break Dick Bong's record were taking a toll on him. And it was obvious to everybody but Tommy McGuire.

The pilot claimed he had never felt better, and the previous weeks' action proved he was not too tired to shoot down Japanese airplanes.

"You are tired, and you won't be rested enough to fly again until I hear that Bong is back in the States and has been greeted as the top-scoring ace in the war."

McGuire listened with a frown on his face. So that was the real reason for grounding him! The general did not want him to steal any of Dick Bong's thunder.

It was true. Kenney—with pressure from Arnold and others—had an alternative motive for preventing Tommy McGuire from becoming the new top-scoring fighter pilot too soon.

"Look, son, as soon as I get the news Dick's back home and has been greeted as the top ace of the war, you can go back to work. If I let you go out today, you are liable to knock off another three Nips like you've done the last two days. That would spoil Dick's whole party and make him far less valuable as a morale and war bond salesman. He would land in San Francisco and have everybody say, 'Hello, Number Two. How's the war going?'"

McGuire relaxed and smiled. He understood the logic. And there would be plenty of targets out there when he was again airborne.

He agreed to take a break. A short one.

Bong arrived back in the United States on January 6, 1945, Philippines time. One of the things Dick had promised McGuire before he left was that he would contact Tommy's wife, Marilynn, and assure her he was doing fine. And tell her he had met with General Kenney again and been promised a long leave Stateside in February. No doubt this time. He would be coming home.

But Dick was not to mention to her all the talk that was going around about how Tommy was to soon become the next to receive the Medal of Honor. That was true, too. Kenney was going to submit the paperwork for the award based on the previous few days' action. And that, of course, would assure his homecoming in February would be permanent, so they could start their life together. McGuire wanted to share the news with her after it was all a bit more solid.

When Kenney received confirmation that Bong had arrived in the US to a true hero's welcome, he invited Tommy McGuire to dinner. There, he told him he could return to the party, but he ordered him to take it easy, not to try to get to forty-one the first day back on the job. If he started pressing, his luck would run out and the general would have to write one of the kinds of letters to parents and wives that he especially hated to compose.

Tommy happily agreed.

The next day, McGuire and three other P-38s lifted off, bound for the island of Negros to look for targets. They saw nothing and were considering starting home when they spotted a single enemy fighter at low altitude. It had likely just taken off from one of the few remaining enemy landing strips down there. Tommy and his wingman dived on the lone target while the other two pilots, recent arrivals, stayed back to watch how the experienced guys did their thing.

What followed was one bit of bad luck after another. The Japanese pilot, who should never have known what hit him, did spy the two Lightnings coming his way. As it turned out, this was no recent rookie replacement Japanese pilot, but a seasoned and skillful instructor. He made a sudden, shrewd, unexpected move, and as McGuire's wingman completely overshot his target, the enemy pilot quickly put himself right on the American's tail and opened fire at close range. The wingman was on the radio, begging McGuire for help as bullets ripped into his P-38, ricocheting off the steel armor at his back.

Tommy swung around hard to go rescue his buddy. However, in the process, he completely forgot to jettison his two practically full auxiliary fuel tanks. With that heavy load still in place beneath each wing, and with the sharp turn and deep dive McGuire was trying to make, it immediately became impossible for him to control the plane. The Lightning went into a tumbling spin, and without enough altitude for Tommy to try to pull out and regain control, it bored right into the muddy ground of the island below, exploding in fire. McGuire died instantly. The man who once told a radio interviewer, "Hunting Japs is the most dangerous hunting of all," was gone.

Native Filipinos eventually located the wreckage and recovered McGuire's body. It was later returned to the United States and buried at Arlington National Cemetery across the Potomac River from Washington, DC. There is today a memorial to McGuire located at the crash site on Negros.

Thomas Buchanan McGuire later received the Medal of Honor posthumously. McGuire Air Force Base in Burlington County, New Jersey, was named for him.

He is still recognized as his country's number two ace fighter pilot, officially credited with thirty-eight kills.

CHAPTER TWENTY-SIX

"HE CAN BE OF GREAT VALUE TO US HERE"

George Kenney described the loss of Tommy McGuire as "one of the worst blows I took in the war." He called the crash of McGuire's P-38 an "accident," since no enemy bullet hit him that day. Nor had a single bullet struck any of the various Lightnings named *Pudgy* he had piloted in all the torrid action in which he had been involved. McGuire was just that good.

"I don't believe there was a Jap in the world that could have shot Tommy down," Kenney wrote. Clearly, the general was reluctant to consider that he might have kept McGuire in the game too long. Or that he might have just gotten lucky in keeping Dick Bong around as long as he did.

However, there had been an incident just before Bong's departure from the Philippines and the heartrending loss of McGuire that gave Kenney reason to believe he was evacuating the kid just in the nick of time. Between the time the general took his P-38 away from Dick and the day he left for home, Kenney asked Bong to do him one more favor. The general wanted him to fly escort for him and his B-17, using a borrowed Lightning, on a quick trip from Tacloban to San Jose, Mindoro. The real reason was because Kenney knew Dick wanted to say farewell to all his friends, many of whom were by then based at San Jose. This quick and relatively safe excursion would give the kid that opportunity. Another opportunity to fly a P-38 in a combat zone, too, but with little chance he would encounter an enemy fighter.

As Kenney fully expected, they saw no Japanese aircraft on the flight over. However, shortly after Dick exited the cockpit and was happily greeting buddies who had come out to congratulate him on the record and to say goodbye, the air raid warning suddenly blared. Bong stood stock-still and watched with an odd look on his face as the pilots on alert raced out, climbed into waiting P-38s, and flew off to intercept the approaching attackers. As Kenney looked on, he could sense how much his star longed to be going up there with them. But the general would have chased down and tackled the kid had he made a break for the P-38.

At least they had a good view of the action. The confrontation took place almost directly above them, well within sight of the base. Bong just stood there, taking it all in as one of the Lightning jockeys scored a direct hit on an Oscar, setting it afire. Then the enemy pilot—obviously without a parachute, as so often was the case—climbed from the blazing cockpit and jumped out to escape the flames. He fell to his death, hitting the runway not more than a hundred feet from where Kenney and Bong watched.

"I had predicted a long while ago that if he ever found out he was not shooting clay pigeons, I would have to take him out of combat," Kenney later wrote. "This was a nice kid. He was no killer, and his pet peeve against the newspapermen was that they kept referring to him as the pilot with 'the most kills.' I believe this was the first time Dick Bong realized that he had been responsible for many similar occurrences."

Kenney bided his time as the kid ran over to some bushes at the edge of the airfield and "for the next five minutes was violently ill."

"I stood there waiting, more convinced than ever that tonight was the time for Dick to start home," Kenney concluded. "He was no longer the happy-go-lucky, snub-nosed, towheaded country boy. This was a rough, dirty game he had been playing, and I instinctively sensed that he didn't want any more of it."

The general was also aware that Dick Bong still had plenty more to offer in service to his country. Just not in combat.

The kid rode back to Tacloban on the B-17 with Kenney. There he would catch the midnight transport for the first leg of his trip home. He left the borrowed P-38 behind at Mindoro for the pilots there to use since the aircraft were still scarce. On the way back to his headquarters that day, the general explained to Dick that he was once again sending a letter with him for Hap Arnold. By doing so, Dick would be designated as a courier and get top priority all along the way. He did not mention to Bong that maybe being a courier would be enough to get him Stateside and in front of all the press and praise before Tommy McGuire inevitably managed to shatter the kid's record-breaking total.

In that letter, he requested that Arnold grant Bong enough

leave time to go home, marry Marge, and have a nice honeymoon. After that, Dick was to report to Wright Field in Dayton, Ohio, and learn all he could about jet engines and jet-powered aircraft. That technology might still be required to win the current war and would certainly be a deterrent to or a powerful weapon in winning the next one. From there, Kenney was asking that Dick and Mrs. Bong be dispatched to Burbank, California, where he would be attached to the Lockheed plant as a test pilot. His job would be to help get the new P-80 Shooting Star jet fighter ready for use in the real world of aerial combat.

That way, he could continue to be a factor in possibly bringing the war to a close sooner. Not by shooting down enemy planes, though. By helping develop weaponry that could ultimately be a factor in defeating the enemy.

Bong had mixed feelings about the idea. He had mostly flown only the P-38 since training. He knew little about the new jets but was eager and willing to learn. He just did not want to let General Kenney down if he was not able to pick up on the technical aspect of the radically new weaponry. After all, his only formal education had been two years of general studies at Superior State. No engineering training at all.

The general scoffed. He was confident a natural pilot like Major Bong could put the P-80 through its paces just fine. And show the engineers exactly what they needed to make it do in order to more effectively overcome enemy air forces, current and future. Do it just as well as his beloved Lightnings had done.

It is noteworthy that Kenney included in his missive to Hap Arnold a comment about whether Bong deserved credit for all his shoot-downs. "In spite of a suggestion made recently in *Time* magazine," he wrote, "none of the official Nips to Bong's credit were setups. He has invariably been selected the leader of the enemy formation in order to break up the show and make it easier for his wingmen to add to their scores. He has more than deserved every one of the decorations he wears."

Kenney ended his letter by admitting to Arnold that the primary reason he was sending Richard Bong home was because he could no longer "take the chance of a loss of morale that would result in case he became a casualty."

It is an even stronger demonstration of how much the USAAF's top man in the Pacific thought of that particular pilot—a favorite since he had first blown the lady's laundry off the clothesline back in San Francisco—that Kenney came down to the airfield at midnight to see Dick off. He also managed to find six bottles of Coca-Cola for him to enjoy on the long flight.

Richard Bong left the war for the final time on December 29, 1944. Being a courier did help speed along his transit. He landed in San Francisco on New Year's Eve and would usher in 1945 aboard another plane bound for Washington, DC.

Bong's homecoming this time was an even bigger media circus than the previous two had been. America was hungry for good news and heroes to worship. And this one continued to occupy the top on the kill leaderboard. Newsreels in movie theaters documented Bong's arrival. Pictures of him were in almost every newspaper and magazine across the country. Many showed him in his dress uniform with the Medal of Honor dangling from his neck. But this time, when Dick first arrived in San Francisco and faced the shouting reporters and constantly popping flash-bulbs, the most often asked questions were not about how he had shot down all those Oscars and Zeros or how much longer he thought the Japanese could hold out. No, they were "Is Major McGuire going to catch you?" and "When are you and Marge going to get married?"

Bong could not yet answer either question. He had accepted the fact that Tommy McGuire would get more enemy planes, and likely in the next week or so. And he did not really care.

He and Marge had not even had a chance yet to discuss the details of their wedding. But with a quick long-distance tele-phone conversation before he left San Francisco for Washington, they got that matter settled. It would be Saturday, February 3, at the Lutheran church in Superior. (That would later be moved to February 10, as their mothers felt they would need more time to get it all together.) Then he wired Marge a bouquet of flowers to seal the deal.

There was another important chore he needed to take care of once he was Stateside. That was to fill his promise to Tommy McGuire to call Marilynn and assure her that her husband was doing fine and that he would for sure be home in February. General Kenney had promised, and he was a man of his word. He found Marilynn mightily incredulous, not a fan of George Kenney, and quite bitter. She had heard that pledge far too many times to believe it now. But Dick had done Kenney's bidding. He wished her well and climbed on the plane headed east.

After visiting with General Arnold ("I had a long talk with [Bong] and I think you are right in sending [him] home," Arnold later replied to Kenney. "He can be of great value to us here."), Dick left Washington with enough leave to last him and Marge until April 6, 1945. On that day, he was to report to Wright Field in Dayton and begin learning about the jets.

Dick had been home in Poplar three days when he heard about the death of Tommy McGuire. Bong's milestone was no longer in immediate jeopardy. He told Marge he was afraid Tommy died trying too hard to break his record. Now somebody besides McGuire would have to do it. Dick hoped nobody else would lose his life in the effort.

Marge graduated from college at the end of January, and she was certified to be a teacher. A few days later, she and Dick drove down to Milwaukee for some obligatory appearances. Headlines on the front page of the *Milwaukee Sentinel* proclaimed, "Milwaukee Gives Hero's Welcome to Major Bong" and "Throngs Line City Streets to Greet Top Ace." At one event, Marge was presented with a thousand-dollar fur coat. She was grateful, since the temperature that day never made it up to 20 degrees.

Concordia Lutheran Church in Superior was packed for the wedding the evening of February 10, and hundreds more waited outside in the freezing cold for a glimpse of the war hero and his beautiful bride. So did representatives of practically every news service, radio network, and publication. Several radio stations, including WLS in Chicago, broadcast the short service live. Dick wore his only dress uniform for the ceremony. With all the command appearances since coming home, it was beginning to get threadbare.

Dick and Marge spent their first night as husband and wife

in a hotel in Minneapolis, the first stop on their leisurely drive to California. Even on their honeymoon, Dick made time to speak to pilot trainees at Tulare, where he had once been a student, and took his new wife up for a ride in one of the AT-6 Texan trainers, just like the one he had once flown during pilot training. They also spent a few days at Sequoia National Park, visited with film stars on movie sets in Hollywood, and were in the audience for and acknowledged by several national network radio broadcasts, which included another encounter with Bing Crosby. Then, while visiting at Lockheed Aircraft in Burbank, his soon-to-be billet, Dick had the opportunity to have Marge squeeze into the cockpit of a P-38 with him and take her up for a spin. She enjoyed the ride, even when Dick did some rolls and dives. She told reporters she had never been afraid. Not with the best pilot in the Army Air Forces on the stick.

All along, Dick tried as best he could to keep up with the progress of the war, both back in the Pacific and in Europe. He heard that General Kenney had moved his HQ to Luzon already. And by the end of February, Allied missions were being flown out of Clark Field—the same airfield that had belonged to the enemy and that had been a primary target while Dick Bong was there.

Russia had liberated Hungary in Europe and their troops were marching toward Berlin. American troops landed on a tiny island in the Pacific named Iwo Jima on February 19 and raised the iconic flag on Mount Suribachi four days later, but they would not fully control the island for another month. By the end of February, a new government had been installed in the Philippines, and Manila was declared fully liberated on March 3. Back in Europe, US Army soldiers crossed the border into Germany on March 7.

Clearly, Hitler was in his final days. So, then, was the war in Europe. Indeed, he would commit suicide on April 30. That was about a month after Bong and his wife reported to Wright Field and set up housekeeping in their first home in the little town of Osborn—now a part of Fairborn, Ohio—not far from the end of one of the longer runways at Wright Field. That runway near their front yard had been recently made longer to accommodate the B-36 "Peacemaker" strategic bombers. The B-36 was being developed specifically to be able to carry a new but very heavy weapon of some kind, one that was veiled in deep, deep secrecy.

Germany would officially surrender on May 8, while Dick and Marge were settling into their home and as Dick began learning about an entirely different kind of airplane.

In the Pacific, the Allies were generally in agreement that they would have to march island by island the rest of the way to the shores of the Japanese Home Islands. Then there would necessarily be an all-out invasion, similar to D-day in France one year prior, but expected to be even more challenging. It would be dubbed Operation Downfall. Estimates were that trying to bring the war to an end through invasion would cost millions of lives across both sides. It appeared, though, to be the only way to accomplish that goal. A devastating firebombing campaign had annihilated more than five dozen major Japanese cities but neither the emperor nor his military leaders had blinked. The invasion forces were tentatively set to go ashore on the southernmost Home Island of Kyushu on November 1, 1945.

However, unbeknownst to the Bongs—and to most anybody

else—research had begun way back in 1939 to develop a radical new type of weapon. One the Allies feared was also being created by both the Germans and the Japanese. Some military leaders saw this radical new bomb as a better way to bring the Empire of Japan to its knees without a deadly invasion and hand-to-hand carnage. In 1943, in the New Mexico desert, work had been done on more rapidly building and testing such a weapon. Soon tentative plans were being made to use it to try to end the war far more quickly and with less human cost than by launching a D-day–type beach landing.

By the end of 1944, even as Richard Bong was having his greatest success as a fighter pilot in the Philippines, the USAAF was busy in Utah making final plans for a combat group capable of delivering two of the newly created weapons from a location in the Pacific to their utilization over targets in Japan.

In April 1945, as the Bongs wrapped up their extended honeymoon and got themselves settled in Ohio, a meeting was convened in Washington to choose the potential targets for the horrific new bombs and to make preliminary plans for their use. All this preparation was in an effort to conceal one of the most closely held secrets in military history.

Of course, nobody could have known that the deployment of the first atomic bomb on Hiroshima, Japan, on August 6, 1945, would somehow be forever linked with the fate of America's top ace fighter pilot, Major Richard Ira Bong.

CHAPTER TWENTY-SEVEN

"QUITE AN AIRPLANE"

Dick Bong need not have worried about his ability to understand jet-powered aircraft, even though he had no engineering education. It came naturally to him, as did most anything else associated with aeronautics. Whether a plane was driven through the sky by propellers and piston motors or by a turbojet engine, if it had wings, Dick could figure it out. Soon he was the one giving the lectures at Wright. And he was enthusiastic about being able to climb into the cockpit of a Shooting Star and put the aircraft through its paces. Maybe even engaging in some mock dogfights with some Lightnings and P-51 Mustangs to see if that thing should even be labeled a fighter plane.

By April and May of 1945, Wright Field had become the Army Air Forces' top aircraft test facility. Though it had at first been blandly named the Flight Test Section of the USAAF Matériel Command, exciting work was being done there, and many of the Army's top pilots, along with civilian test pilots—many of whom had significant combat experience—were a major part of the effort. Dick soon felt right at home.

The first week of June, almost two months to the day after their arrival in Dayton, the Bongs piled all their possessions into the new car they had purchased and once again hit the road. They veered north to make a quick visit with family in Poplar and Superior before following much of Route 66 west. Along the way, they almost certainly talked of their future. Dick had written home and said he did not know if he would remain in the Army or not when his reenlistment came up late in 1945. There were many aircraft companies on the West Coast, and a civilian test pilot could make good money while keeping a reasonably normal work schedule. Any of those companies would certainly have a place for the country's top ace and Medal of Honor recipient. It was a dangerous job, of course, but not in the same league as exchanging .50-caliber gunfire with a Zero in the skies over New Guinea. It would keep Dick flying, though. Whether he was in the Army or a civilian, in California or back in Wisconsin, flying was what he wanted to do for the rest of his life.

Once they arrived in California, they would encounter the same problem many other military families were having at the time. Housing was hard to come by. And expensive when it was available.

The couple finally settled on a tiny place in Hollywood and moved in in mid-July. Though it was cramped, Dick told the folks back home it was far better than a tent in Dobodura, New Guinea, or a hut shared with a bunch of other sweaty pilots in Tacloban in the Philippines. Though they agreed this would certainly not be their "forever home," Marge went to work decorating the bungalow as Dick went off to work every day. He might just as well have been going to a nine-to-five office job as far as Marge was concerned. For security reasons, he could not tell her much about what he did each day or about the new kind of airplane he was flying. She suspected that what he did each day involved considerably more risk than simply navigating the relatively new Los Angeles freeways to the "office."

Everyone who mattered agreed the country's top ace was more than capable of test flying the P-80s that were just coming off the assembly line in Burbank, ready to be vetted. He was, after all, a natural-born pilot. But the bird he would be flying had already proven to be problematic. In early experimental flights, the plane had become the first jet to break 500 miles per hour. However, a test pilot had died in a crash of a Shooting Star in October of 1944 when the main fuel pump failed at a crucial point in the flight, during takeoff. Another pilot had died in a crash in England in January 1945 while demonstrating the plane there. Yet another flier had just managed to bail out but was injured in March 1945 when a rotor blade broke and the plane's engine disintegrated. That incident had occurred in Burbank just a few days after the Bongs visited Lockheed and Dick had given Marge that thrill ride in a P-38.

Even so, by the summer of 1945, the P-80 was in full production and considered by Lockheed and the USAAF to be reliable and safe. Or as safe as any vehicle that went more than 500 miles per hour could be. Dick Bong reasoned he had seen engines fail and other systems go whacky on plenty of P-38s, and the Lightning was about as good an airplane as there had ever been.

Dick flew the P-80 for the first time on July 7, three days

after he and Marge had sat in the grass at the Rose Bowl and watched the spectacular fireworks light up the sky in celebration of Independence Day. He was impressed with the jet. He wrote home telling his family that the Shooting Star was "quite an airplane all right."

August 6 was to be a big day for Dick. He was scheduled to give a recently constructed P-80 its checkout flight. That was a relatively routine run through the Southern California skies to make sure all systems were performing properly on the plane before it was to be shuttled out to wherever it would be used by the USAAF. He had been invited by Bing Crosby, who had become a friend, to accompany him in a round of golf that afternoon. However, when Dick arrived at Lockheed that morning, he realized he had forgotten his golf shoes at home. He called Bing's office and canceled.

The plane he was to fly that day was a P-80A version, the fifty-sixth one that had rolled off the nearby assembly line. Lockheed would eventually turn out almost 600 of them to be used by the Air Force and Navy, including in the Korean War. This specific airplane already had a couple of hours of flight time on it, and all appeared fine. It would be Bong's twelfth flight in a Shooting Star, and he already felt comfortable in its cockpit.

He took off at two thirty p.m. and, according to some who were watching from the ground, climbed much more quickly than was typical. As he accelerated past 100 miles per hour, the plane abruptly turned to the right at a surprisingly sharp angle—again based on observations from the ground—and was at 200 feet altitude.

An experienced pilot on the ground and a Lockheed mechanic were both watching the takeoff. They reported seeing some black smoke from the rear of the jet. A nearby resident was in her backyard when she heard the plane approaching. Living where she did, she was quite familiar with the sounds of the engines, including the new jet aircraft. This one sounded different to her. The motor was making what she would later tell United Press International sounded like popping. And the wings were wobbling as the plane seemed to be losing altitude. Then, worst of all, she could clearly see the pilot standing up in the cockpit and then jumping out of the plane.

Then there was an explosion. Debris flew everywhere.

Marge heard news of the crash almost immediately on the radio. She called Lockheed but could not get anyone who knew anything on the phone. She knew Dick was flying that day. She also knew another test pilot was to take a plane up that afternoon, too. But she learned the worst when an Air Forces representative knocked on her door. He was followed shortly by a newspaper reporter. Then, minutes later, a bevy of media people. Flashbulbs were exploding. Microphones were shoved into her face while reporters shouted inane questions. One even asked her if she was pregnant.

Back in Wisconsin, the Bongs heard the news the same way Marge had. But by then, it had been confirmed that it was American hero pilot Richard Bong, the Medal of Honor recipient, who had died in the crash soon after takeoff. The Bongs called the Vattendahls to tell them the horrible news. Then there was nothing to do but try to reckon with how a man who had survived all the Japanese had hurled at him could die in a perfectly good airplane near Hollywood.

It was already the next day when General George Kenney heard the news. He was about to leave an airstrip on Okinawa, which had been taken only six weeks before.

"He had met the best the Japanese Air Force could send against him for more than two years and had won," he later wrote. "But now he had joined the long list of gallant airmen whose brilliant careers had been terminated by accident."

There is a good chance that Dick Bong remained a hero until the very end. His body was located about a hundred feet from where the P-80A hit the ground. It disintegrated within a huge ball of fire near Satsuma Avenue and Oxnard Street in a tightly packed residential community. Clearly, when he tried to eject, Dick's parachute had not had time to deploy. Bong died instantly when he hit the ground.

But there was something else. It appeared he had lingered in the cockpit of the stricken aircraft longer than he should have. Once Dick realized he could not save the plane, he managed to steer it and keep it airborne until he saw it would come down in a narrow stretch of cleared ground that served as a power company right-of-way. He had somehow kept it away from any of the nearby crowded neighborhoods, avoiding a far worse catastrophe.

Evening papers that day carried the sad news of the loss of one of America's best-known and admired heroes. But there, next to the Bong story, on the front pages and above the folds of papers across America, were still more bold headlines about the day's other major news event.

At the top of the front page of the August 7 edition of the morning *Los Angeles Times*, there were two banner headlines: "Atomic Bomb Hits Japan" and just below it, in only a slightly smaller font, "Jet Plane Explosion Kills Maj. Bong."

"It was obvious the curly-headed winner of the Congressional Medal of Honor, and the 'hottest' combat pilot in the nation's history, was dead," the accompanying story about Dick Bong read. It also made note of the fact that he was only twenty-four years old.

Under the Hiroshima headline, an Associated Press story read, "The most terrible destructive force ever harnessed by man—atomic energy released by the disintegration of uranium—is now being turned on the islands of Japan by United States bombers. The Japanese face the threat of utter desolation and their capitulation may be greatly speeded up."

Again, war led to technological innovation as well as to the emergence of many unexpected heroes. And though Dick Bong did not live to see it, the United States had found a way to accomplish his primary goal every time he lifted off in his P-38 Lightning.

They had done what they believed was necessary to shorten a terrible war.

EPILOGUE

"[Major Bong] stands in the unbroken line of patriots who have dared to die that freedom might live. And grow. And increase its blessings," read a release from President Harry Truman, the man who ultimately authorized the deployment of the atomic bombs on Hiroshima and Nagasaki after the death of Franklin Roosevelt. "Freedom lives. And through it, he lives—in a way that humbles the undertakings of most men."

Astronaut Frank Borman would later tell Marge Bong that he was confident Dick would have been chosen as one of the original members of the nation's first manned spaceflight program, Project Mercury. He maintained that Dick had had exactly what they were looking for. That was probably a stretch. As with fellow war hero and test pilot Chuck Yeager, a lack of formal education would probably have disqualified Richard Bong from becoming an astronaut.

General Hap Arnold wrote a letter to Marge in which he said, "All the atomic bombs in the world can never make up for loss of men like your husband. Dick was a true hero, modest in achievement, clean-cut, with the stature of an outstanding American."

That "outstanding American's" body was flown aboard a USAAF C-54 Skymaster back to Duluth, Minnesota. Marge Vattendahl Bong had a seat on the same plane. Estimates were that more than a thousand people were there to welcome him— and her—home.

The funeral was held on August 8 at Concordia Lutheran Church, the same place where Dick and Marge had been married almost exactly six months before. The service was led by Reverend Paul Boe, the same minister who had overseen the couple's nuptial vows back in February.

Bong was buried in Plat I, Block 8, Lot 10, Grave 2, of Poplar Cemetery in Douglas County, Wisconsin.

Back in California, all P-80s were grounded while the cause of Bong's crash was investigated. It was determined that the same failure that had led to the death of the first test pilot the previous year had caused this accident. No one was ever able to find out what precisely had gone wrong, even though other pilots attempted to re-create all the same parameters. "Loss of fuel pressure" was the final cryptic description of the cause of the crash.

It would be many years later before Marge was agreeable to attending public events associated with her husband. That was when she went to the dedication of a bridge to be named for and dedicated to Dick, on US Highway 2 across the St. Louis River, connecting Duluth and Superior. Even then, she went only because the Bong family urged her to do so.

The Bongs repeatedly told her that even though her time with Dick had been so short, she would always be a member of the family. After the bridge dedication, her attitude changed dramatically. She became enthusiastic about attending other events, primarily as an advocate for veterans and their families. She spoke often to large and enthusiastic crowds at aviation and veterans' conventions and gatherings. Her daughter later said, "She was a rock star."

After Dick's death, Marge enjoyed a long career as a painter, fashion model, and magazine publisher, including editing a magazine for enthusiasts of the boxer dog breed. She remarried in 1946 but was divorced shortly after. She then met and married fashion-trade magazine editor Murray Drucker, with whom she had two daughters. He passed away in 1991.

Until the bridge dedication in October 1985, few knew she was the widow of a World War II hero. Even her daughters say they knew little of her previous life because she was reluctant to talk about it. But once she became active in veterans' causes, she was instrumental in the establishment of Richard I. Bong Veterans Historical Center in Superior. However, she was adamant that its name and exhibits not only include her former husband but also be dedicated to veterans of all wars. She later wrote, "People have often asked me what Richard would have thought about the heritage center. I always explain that I think he would have been very upset if this was just for him. But the heritage center brings in all veterans, all aspects of the war."

Marge sold her home of fifty years in the Hollywood Hills and moved back to the Bong family farm in Poplar before her death from breast cancer on September 27, 2003. Her ashes are buried next to Dick in Poplar Cemetery.

Her obituary in the *Duluth News Tribune* noted, "Over the past two decades, Marjorie dedicated her time to ensuring that the stories of veterans would not be forgotten. She was the vice-chair of the Richard I. Bong Veterans Historical Center and an active speaker on behalf of World War II veterans. Known for her quick wit and sense of humor, she loved talking to WWII veterans and hearing their stories."

In addition to the museum and bridge in Superior and Richard Bong State Recreation Area in Kenosha County, Wisconsin, Richard Bong's name is on the airport in Superior; a bridge in Townsville, Australia; theaters in Misawa, Japan, and at Hickam Air Force Base in Hawaii; and streets and avenues at Lackland Air Force Base in San Antonio, Texas; at Luke Air Force Base in Glendale, Arizona; at Elmendorf Air Force Base in Anchorage, Alaska; at Fairchild Air Force Base in Spokane, Washington; at Kadena Air Force Base in Okinawa, Japan; at Barksdale Air Force Base in Bossier City, Louisiana; and in Dayton, Ohio, on the street leading to the National Museum of the United States Air Force.

Construction began in Wisconsin in mid-1954 on what was to be Richard I. Bong Air Force Base. But then, three days before concrete was to be poured for a 12,500-foot runway, the Air Force abruptly and without comment halted and abandoned the project. The land cleared for the runway is still visible from the air. The site was eventually turned over to the state and most of it ultimately became Richard Bong State Recreation Area.

Prior to that, there was a plan to name Spokane Air Force Base in Washington State after Bong. However, when Air Force General Muir Fairchild, a native of Bellingham, Washington, died while on duty, the decision was made to name the facility Fairchild Air Force Base.

Both decisions came as a disappointment to the Bong family. But they knew Dick would probably have appreciated just as much having the recreation area named for him. Hunting is supposed to be exceptionally good there.

In addition to her accepting the Bong family's invitation to attend the bridge-naming ceremony in Duluth, there was another incident that helped Marge accept her legacy.

She often told the story of shopping in a toy store with one of her grandchildren. The child came running to her, excitedly showing her a box found on a nearby shelf. It was an airplane model kit, similar to the ones Dick had built as a child, but this one depicted a World War II P-38 Lightning. It was *Marge*, Dick's plane. The picture on the outside of the box clearly showed Marge's college graduation picture and her name on the nose of the model.

Marge would later say that was the moment she fully realized that she had been a part of history in her previous life. History that she vowed to continue honoring and preserving.

And that she did.

We can hope that this book does some of that, too. And that maybe it will lead to a few more people thinking of a brave young fighter pilot rather than a glass pipe when they pass that sign along I-94 at exit 340 in southeast Wisconsin.